UNCIVIL YOUTH

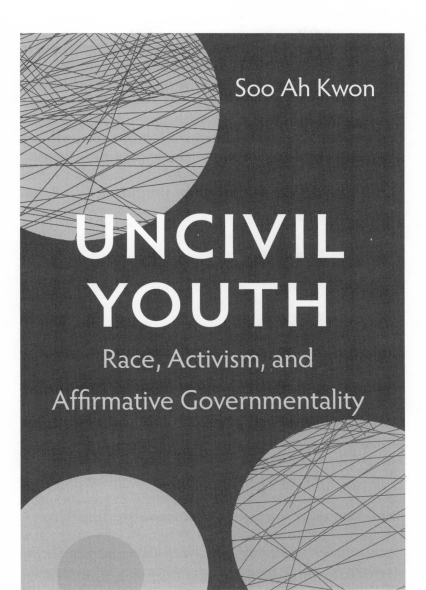

Soo Ah Kwon

UNCIVIL YOUTH

Race, Activism, and
Affirmative Governmentality

DUKE UNIVERSITY PRESS

DURHAM AND LONDON

2013

© 2013 DUKE UNIVERSITY PRESS
All rights reserved
Printed in the United States of America
on acid-free paper ∞
Designed by C. H. Westmoreland
Typeset in Minion Pro with Hypatia Sans Display
by Keystone Typesetting, Inc.

Library of Congress Cataloging-in-Publication Data
Kwon, Soo Ah
Uncivil youth : race, activism, and affirmative governmentality / Soo Ah Kwon.
p. cm.
Includes bibliographical references and index.
ISBN 978-0-8223-5405-5 (cloth : alk. paper)
ISBN 978-0-8223-5423-9 (pbk. : alk. paper)
1. Minorities—Political activity—United States.
2. Youth—Political activity—United States. 3. Nonprofit organizations.
4. Democracy and education—United States. I. Title.
E184.A1K887   2013
305.2350973—dc23   2012044747

FOR MY PARENTS

CONTENTS

Acknowledgments   ix

Introduction   1

CHAPTER 1
Civilizing Youth against Delinquency   27

CHAPTER 2
Youth Organizing and
the Nonprofitization of Activism   45

CHAPTER 3
Organizing against Youth Criminalization   73

CHAPTER 4
Confronting the State   95

Conclusion   121

Notes   131

References   149

Index   165

ACKNOWLEDGMENTS

My deepest appreciation goes to the members of Asian/Pacific Islander Youth Promoting Advocacy and Leadership (AYPAL), who welcomed me into their organization and generously shared their lives with me. I had the opportunity to get to know and learn from many incredible young people during my time with AYPAL. Their sense of humor, quick wit, and ceaseless energy devoted to organizing for social justice have deeply affected my way of seeing and thinking about the world. I am especially grateful to the amazing group of staff organizers who served as my second family. I have so much admiration and respect for all of them; I wish I could name them here and give them the recognition they deserve. Their passion and commitment to working with young people to challenge social injustice is truly remarkable.

I was fortunate to have worked with outstanding colleagues and faculty members who saw me through the beginnings of this book at the University of California, Berkeley. I grew as a scholar in the company, collaboration, and friendship of a spectacular cohort: Andrea Dyrness, Emma Fuentes, Shabnam Koirala-Azad, Amanda Lashaw, Kysa Nygreen, and Patricia Sanchez. My advisor and unfailing cheerleader Carol Stack deserves special praise for her keen ethnographic eye. I am also grateful to Michael Omi, who provided rich guidance. My deep appreciation goes to Stuart Tannock for offering me the theoretical tools to approach a study of youth.

Many wonderful colleagues and friends offered invaluable support while I was writing this book. I feel privileged to have fellow scholars who so generously took the time and energy to engage with drafts of my manuscript at its various stages: Nancy Abelmann, Ruth Nicole Brown, Sara Clarke-Kaplan, Kirstie Dorr, Maria Gillombardo, Robert Hughes, Robin Jarrett, Reed Larson, Amanda Lashaw, Lisa Nakamura, Fiona Ngô, Mimi Thi Nguyen, and Kent Ono. I am particularly indebted to two exceptional writing partners, Fiona Ngô and Mimi Thi Nguyen, whose sharp intellect and unfailing support were crucial. Mimi's genuine interest and careful read of my work have critically shaped its outcome. Special thanks to Fiona for suggesting the title for this book. I extend appreciation to Yen Le Espiritu and Sunaina Maira for the sage feedback they provided on an early draft of this manuscript. I am also grateful to my anonymous manuscript readers at Duke University Press and their rigorous and thoughtful engagement with my work, from which I benefited immensely. Thanks also to Fay Hodza, Vincent Pham, Melissa Pognon, and Teresa Ramos for their research assistance.

Heartfelt thanks for the support and the good cheer extended by Lisa Marie Cacho, David Coyoca, Aaron Ebata, Augusto Espiritu, Stephen Hocker, Moon-Kie Jung, Susan Koshy, Esther Lee, Christy Lleras, Adrienne Lo, Mireya Loza, Martin Manalansan IV, Brent McBride, Ray McDermott, Isabel Molina, Ramona Oswald, Naomi Paik, Yoon Pak, Marcela Raffaelli, Junaid Rana, Maria Rund, Constance Shapiro, Siobhan Somerville, Ian Sprandel, Elizabeth Sweet, Yutian Wong, and Caroline Yang during the completion of this book. Much gratitude also to all the faculty and staff members in the Department of Asian American studies and the Department of Human and Community Development at the University of Illinois at Urbana-Champaign, who have individually and collectively provided me with so much support. I am grateful to have the benefits of the rich intellectual and social community they sustain.

I am delighted to have found a home for this book at Duke University Press and appreciate the people there who made the publication process a smooth one: Courtney Berger, Christine Choi, Katherine Courtland, Jeanne Ferris, Liz Smith, Cherie Westmoreland, and Ken Wissoker. Thanks to Ken for taking the time to patiently hear my project out. Many thanks to Courtney, an amazing editor, for shepherding my book from the beginning to the very end with unwavering enthusiasm. Grants from the Center for Democracy in a Multiracial Society Fellowship and the Campus Research Board's Humanities Time Release at the University of Illinois at Urbana-Champaign gave me time off from teaching to concentrate on writing. I discuss the case of young people's activism against juvenile hall expansion in chapter 3 in an essay, "Youth of Color Organizing for Juvenile Justice," in *Beyond Resistance! Youth Activism and Community Change*, edited by Shawn Ginwright, Pedro Noguera, and Julio Cammarota (New York: Routledge, 2006), 215–28. An earlier version of chapter 4 was published as "Deporting Cambodian Refugees: Youth Activism, State Reform, and Imperial Statecraft," in *positions* 20, no. 3 (2012): 737–62.

Special recognition goes to my parents and family members who continue to provide steadfast support—never questioning or doubting me. Words cannot express my gratitude for Dustin Allred and our son Max. They provided me with both the necessary break and the inspiration I needed during the writing process. This book would not have been possible without Dustin's daily gestures of kindness and support. Max's enthusiastic and relentless questioning—"What chapter did you work on today?" and "What's taking you so long?"—energized me as I completed the manuscript. A million thanks and love to you both!

INTRODUCTION

In 1996 residents of Oakland, California, passed Measure K, the Kids First! Initiative, which was an amendment to the city charter that set aside 2.5 percent of the city's unrestricted, general-purpose funds toward after-school programs for underserved children and youth. Voter approval of Measure K revived traditional community programs for educational tutoring and drug and violence prevention. But it also provided the impetus for the formation of youth activist groups, such as Asian/Pacific Islander Youth Promoting Advocacy and Leadership (AYPAL), of which I was a volunteer staff member and ethnographer in the early 2000s. Founded in 1998, AYPAL had the mission of promoting social justice, youth community involvement, and youth leadership. It is one of many youth organizations that emerged in the 1990s and that have become a driving force in the new youth organizing movement. Its members were Asian and Pacific Islander youth—ages fourteen to eighteen—from Cambodian, Chinese, Filipino, Korean, Laotian, Mien, Samoan, Tongan, and Vietnamese immigrant and refugee families in Oakland; most of the young people were second-generation immigrants, but some were first-generation.[1]

Nonprofits that organize youth differ from politically neutral youth-based community programs because they explicitly focus on social justice and community organizing strategies. As Mattie Weiss notes, "Fundamentally, youth organizing involves a membership of young people involved in direct action, an analysis of power in society, and recognition of the need for institutional change."[2] Mostly poor, urban, high school–aged youth of color—African American, Asian American, and Latino/a—these young people belong to community-based nonprofit organizations that serve as a support base for their activism.[3]

Increasingly visible since the 1990s, these youth of color have staged direct actions, influenced policy decisions, and mobilized their peers and community members across the United States. Their activism is directed against injustices they encounter in their everyday lives: racial and educational inequality, increasing rates of youth incarceration, and heightened criminalization of young people. For instance, young members of Californians for Justice conducted surveys in their high schools in Long Beach, San Diego, and San Jose to produce a report in 2001 describing unequal school conditions and racial disparities in student educational achievement; the report received statewide news coverage.[4] In Los Angeles, young people of South Central Youth Empowered through Action successfully redirected $153 million in public funding to improve low-income school infrastructure.[5] The youth in AYPAL tackled educational issues of budget cuts, decrepit school facilities, and racial discrimination and harassment in the classroom by successfully pressuring the Oakland school superintendent to institute districtwide school reform policies to address students' concerns.[6] Also during my time with AYPAL, the youth were part of a multiracial youth coalition to stop the expansion of a juvenile detention facility, or juvenile hall, in their neighborhood, a case I discuss in detail in chapter 3. Young people in the South Bronx organized so that juvenile detainees at a detention center could receive high school diplomas.[7]

Although young people's activism is often youth-centered, it also tackles problems faced by the larger community. In a different campaign I also discuss in detail, AYPAL convinced their congressional representative to support ending the deportation of noncitizens convicted of minor or nonviolent crimes. In El Paso, young people of the Border Network for Human Rights documented abuses perpetrated by state authorities at the US-Mexico border. Members of Youth United for Community Action in East Palo Alto fought for environmental justice by organizing against the construction of a hazardous waste facility in their neighborhood.[8]

The issues young people took on must be understood within the larger context of political, social, and economic changes wrought under neoliberalism, starting in the late 1970s. Youth opposed policies to monopolize and privatize public resources, the devolution of social programs and public education, and increased state militarization, changes that greatly affected poor working-class families, immigrants, and communities of color. California voters, for instance, were faced with a barrage of propositions in the 1990s (184, 187, 209, 227, and 21), which disproportionately meted severe criminal penalties to men of color, curtailed public social services in education and employment, made scapegoats of the state's immigrant populations, and punished young people. Much of the community activism in the late twentieth and early twenty-first centuries was against local anti-immigration and racist voter initiatives of this time, but activists also opposed larger economic conditions resulting from neoliberal policies.[9] Furthermore, young people's activism challenged increased state militarization following the launch of the war on terror and the US invasion of Afghanistan and Iraq in the aftermath of September 11, 2001. The US government response to the attacks incited a strong antiwar movement in the Bay Area and across the country, and AYPAL youth marched against the invasions along with a hundred thousand other protestors.

The initiative most directly affecting young people, and what many of the youth and adult organizers I worked with identified as the mobilizing impetus among youth of color in California, was Proposition 21, the Gang Violence and Juvenile Crime Prevention Act. This proposition sought more severe penalties for gang-related crimes, proposed that children as young as fourteen be subject to trial as adults, and sought to streamline such trials. Proposition 21 was passed by voters in 2000, but the constitutionality of the measure was contested in the courts. Despite its passage, the legislation was met with much resistance by youth of color, especially in Northern California. For instance, the measure did not pass in Alameda (where Oakland is located) and San Francisco Counties. Although proponents of Proposition 21 justified their arguments for the legislation with mainstream media representations of superviolent youth of color, sometimes referred to as "superpredators," who were in need of punishment and control, these very young people pushed back against the portrayal of themselves as delinquents and troublemakers.[10] A positive and deliberately political youth and youth of color identity linked to resistance and activism emerged to counter this trend in criminalization, emphasizing racial identity and opposition to youth criminalization as central concepts in the youth organizing movement. The phrase "youth of color" stems from organizing among "people of color" of the Third World movements that rallied around familiar experiences of racism and oppression. The Bay Area—and Oakland in particular, as the birthplace of the black power movement—has a long history of organized action against state power. Youth of color organizing thus has intimate ties to these social movements among traditionally marginalized groups, and it shares in a legacy of student activism. However, a distinguishing feature of this youth organizing movement is the participation in it by a large number of high school–aged youth.[11]

As a popular chant heard at many youth organizing events proclaimed, "Ain't no power like the power of the youth, and the power of the youth don't stop!" The chant encapsulates the energy and enthusiasm of this movement. Youth of color organizing as grassroots activism holds special currency in progressive, leftist political circles. Youth organizing is referred to by some as the "new civil rights movement," and its advocates hail young people as central to the revitalization of democracy and the fight for social justice.[12]

This book, however, resists such an unquestioning acceptance of youth activism and instead examines the conditions of possibility that enable "the power of the youth." *Uncivil Youth* is in part a cautionary tale. The impetus for my research stems from my personal experience as a member of AYPAL who saw the power of youth organizing as a strategy for enabling youth of color to become agents of social change. But at times I found problematic the uncritical promotion of these young people as social change leaders. During my fieldwork, and even more so after I left the field, I wondered: What did it mean to promote youth as political actors when they were not of voting age? Why was youth of color organizing centered around and supported by nonprofit organizations? Why was there a sudden focus on youth, who had earlier been commonly understood as apolitical? And why was there such positive attention to youth of color, who were often construed as violent criminals or teenage mothers? In a closer examination of when, how, and why youth organizing came to represent an effective strategy for solving social ills, I began to question the relationship between the state and civil society, specifically the nonprofit organizations that develop and promote youth organizing.

As I elaborate in this book, youth of color organizing and the activist-oriented nonprofits supporting it do result from oppositional social movements of this time, but they also have roots in the efforts of a select group of philanthropic foundations and practitioners that viewed potentially "at-risk" youth of color as worthy agents of community leadership and transformation. Youth of color activism is embedded in strategies to prevent potentially "at-risk" subjects from engaging in the potentially risky behaviors of juvenile crime and sex, by allowing youth to participate in community programs that provide more wholesome supports and opportunities. I explore the previously overlooked relations of power that mediate youth of color organizing—widely celebrated as a "progressive social justice movement"—

and the nonprofit organizations and foundations that support it. Drawing on Michel Foucault's observations about modern democratic governance and its imperative of self-government and self-care, I argue that our political projects must seriously contend with those relations of power that rule through subjectivity and subjection, affirmation and criminalization.[13] Focusing on the youth of color organizing movement and the role of nonprofit organizations that enable, but also direct, this upsurge in young people's activism, I take a closer look at what I call an affirmative governmentality, through which youth organizing operates as a strategy for empowering youth through their voluntary participation in nonprofit organizations.

I take the position that although social justice–oriented nonprofit organizations and the foundations that support them may be not for profit, they are nevertheless subject to capitalism's logics and the neoliberal state's art of governance, just as they may be engaged in practices of opposition. The ostensible independence of civil society and the subsequent idealized view of political organizing as occurring apart from the state rely on particular histories of the development and depoliticization of oppositional movements. The expansion of nonprofits in the latter half of the twentieth century is tied to the steady incorporation and professionalization of activism, evidenced in the legal restrictions of political activities allowed under nonprofit status along with the state's post–civil rights affirmation and transformation of race and racial identities into categories of resource administration. Meanwhile trends of social disinvestment and corporatization overburden public nonprofits that offer social services, while increasingly situating these organizations as important sites of care for marginalized groups. I examine the nonprofitization of activism and the constitution of nonprofits as a technology of neoliberal governance, processes that have severely limited the potential of oppositional political activism in the contemporary moment. It is these collusions and complicities between state and civil society, specifically youth activist nonprofit organizations, that together mediate and manage youth as political actors and democratic subjects that inform the central inquiry of this book.

The phrase "uncivil youth" underscores my concerns with youth of color organizing, which I assert is embedded in neoliberalism's structures of governance. I interrogate the relations of power that both enable and limit young people, particularly racial minority youth, as political actors and emerging democratic subjects, as well as inevitable vectors of danger. This book's title thus marks the portrayal of youth of color as a social threat to be managed through the competing policies of youth empowerment and youth criminalization. It is a theoretical and political investigation of youth of color—specifically, Asian and Pacific Islander youth—as a governmentalized category of intervention in which nonprofit organizations are called on to care for and empower these potentially "at-risk" subjects. But as I will also demonstrate, "uncivil youth" describes young people's practices of civil disobedience and their political activism to challenge modern US governmentality. I focus on forces that constrain youth activism, but I also pay a great deal of attention to the practices of young people to make sense of and oppose the relations of power that produce their marginalization.

My aim in engaging in a critique of youth of color organizing is not to condemn it. I witnessed firsthand, based on my work with AYPAL, countless young people with little inclination toward political participation develop into vocal social activists and leaders, and I saw the power of their collective actions. Rather, my purpose is to carefully attend to the multiple powers of subjectivity and subjection, as well as to the political practices that accept and refuse them. This means to pay attention to how power may affirm, oppress, or operate unrecognized. I resist the wholesale promotion of youth of color as vanguards of social change, but I insist that a critical examination of the advancement of them as political actors is necessary for an understanding of activism today. To interrogate neoliberal political and economic philosophies, and their meanings for democratic citizenship, I rely on feminist political theories that draw on Foucault's theses on the modern art of government.[14] In pursuing these inquiries, I contend that neoliberalism is not totalizing, and that individuals and social movements are continually engaged in exposing the contradictions of its political and ideological hegemony. I situate my work within the scholarship and political legacy of ethnic studies, which couples an investment in the politics of knowledge production about and among minority groups with efforts toward social change.

Affirmative Governmentality and "At-Risk" Youth

To examine the forms of power that promote young people as political actors is to understand the management of them as an important project of the state's care and control. Imagined as crucial to a nation's future, young people are viewed as investments in need of guidance. But their care is also figured in conceptions of them as transitional subjects positioned somewhere between child and adult, requiring particularized governance (anchored in discourses of their physical and social immaturity) and punishment (as perpetrators of crime and loose sexual behavior). Disturbingly, youth of color are not often imagined as future agents of democracy, but as objects already under suspicion and state surveillance and regulation. "Youth" itself frequently suggests negative connotations. Jean and John Comaroff write: "In much of the late-twentieth-century English-speaking world, young white persons are *teenagers*, their black counterparts are *youth*, adolescents with attitude. And most often, if not always, male."[15] Despite a steady overall decrease in youth crime since 1980, youth of color are all too often targets of state crime prevention measures, as exemplified by the institution of antigang task forces in California's Street Terrorism Enforcement and Prevention Act of 1988 and Proposition 21 in 2000. Add to this the imposition of curfews, assignment of police officers to patrol schools, mass arrests for petty crimes such as loitering, heightened penalties for drug trafficking, and the trying of juvenile offenders as adults. Nationally, minority youth are more likely than white youth to be arrested, detained, referred, and tried in juvenile courts—and they are more likely to receive harsher punishments, including detention in adult state prisons.[16] African Americans, American Indians, Latino/as, and a growing number of Asian Americans and Pacific Islanders make up the majority of young people locked up in juvenile hall. Since 1980 female incarceration rates have steadily doubled every seven to eight years, and one-third of the juveniles arrested in 2003 were young women.[17] Female youth, however, are more likely than their male counterparts to be arrested for status offenses— offenses committed only by juveniles—and suspected immoral sexual conduct (including running away, prostitution, and what is known as incorrigibility).[18] Despite this spike in female incarceration, youth crime and delinquency is coded as masculine—more precisely, the young delinquent is seen as a male who is also a racial minority. This not only reflects the traditional management of young men for so-called delinquent, antisocial acts but also of young women for suspected acts of sexual immorality.

These youth (often poor, minority, and urban) are constructed and understood as an "at-risk" population in need of intervention, whether that takes the form of care or punishment. Yet in the current moment, certain populations, such as the homeless and "dangerous" youth, are no longer deemed "at-risk." Rather, they are considered inevitable risks in themselves, and their physical banishment or punishment is thus legitimated by the state before they even engage in delinquent behavior or commit a crime.[19] These surplus subjects lie "outside of risk" and therefore beyond the normalizing technologies of reform and programs of a neoliberal state.[20] Most often, as Lisa Marie Cacho explains, African American and Latino/a youth serve as markers of social deviancy and are already marked as devalued and unworthy subjects of care.[21] The youth of color I worked with, and countless other participants in groups sponsored by youth organizing nonprofits, were situated at this slippery intersection. They were members of an "at-risk" population who might yet be enabled to become entrepreneurial self-empowered subjects, but they also teetered close to those "outside of risk." Thus, the neoliberal state and its technologies of affirmation and punishment are closely involved in the lives of youth of color. The state is both caring and ruthless in its approach to "at-risk" youth of color. In other words, powers that promote youth empowerment are not separate from those of youth criminalization.

Since the nineteenth century, civil society and its institutions have targeted marginalized youth as a special category of intervention through after-school, community-based programs, which have been posed as a preventive solution to young people's probable delinquency and sexual immorality. In a historical study of after-school youth programs since the Progressive Era, Robert Halpern notes: "From the outset, after-school proponents linked their work to prevention of problems, especially crime and delinquency."[22] Chapter 1 situates contemporary youth of color organizing as the latest youth intervention strategy arising from this tradition, aimed at transforming poor, immigrant, and minority youth to become better democratic subjects. I examine two cornerstones of youth services—after-school programs and the juvenile justice system—to make my argument about those commensurate forms of power that produce young people through subjectivity and subjection. Participation in wholesome community-based programs continues to be offered today with this implicit, if not explicit, purpose: as this story goes, involvement in such programs will steer poor youth of color onto an alternative path of responsible citizenship, away from those dangers (drugs, gangs, prison, sexual disease, and pregnancy) assumed to otherwise loom close at hand for these youth. Too often such prevention measures are offered as ways to control male criminality and female sexuality, through which youth of color are already marked as deviant. For young people of color construed as a vulnerable but also threatening "at-risk" population, becoming a good citizen-subject necessitates voluntarily and willingly (and, I might add, enthusiastically) participating in supervised programs designed to empower them. Failure to participate may be used to justify state interventions and legitimate young people's criminalization and punishment.

Nonprofit youth organizations charged with improving the life chances of "at-risk" youth of color are directly linked to the modern state and the reconfiguration of civil society as a technology of neoliberal citizenship. Foucault argues that civil society, while assumed to be a domain separate from the state, is very much a "concept of governmental technology" that mediates the development of self-governing entrepreneurial subjects in a capitalist state.[23] I contend that nonprofit organizations are called upon to regulate as well as to empower "at-risk" young people to exercise responsibility and self-government in what I call an affirmative governmentality. My concept of affirmative governmentality is not so much a departure from Foucault as it is an elaboration on his ideas. Governmentality for Foucault describes a system of liberal governance. Governmentality names the relationships and practices of power through which citizens and populations are subject to control and exercise that control on themselves.[24] Foucault notes that the key to liberalism is the state's restrained exercise of police power and the practice of the art of government of "self-limitation."[25] Governance in a liberal democracy is not an exercise of absolute state power (although it is not bereft of that power), and therefore neither are the practices that make up acts of citizenship. In other words, the relations of power within democratic liberal governance are as much about enabling its subjects to govern themselves—and enlisting their willing participation in the process.[26]

Neoliberalism increases this shift in the art of government to render the individual as governmentalizable in a new fashion, one that is steeped in economic rationales. Contrary to liberal political thought that categorizes market forces as separate from the state, the neoliberal state, in Foucault's view, is mutually constitutive of the economy. It is "a state under the supervision of the market rather than a market supervised by the state."[27] Importantly in such a configuration, market values and reasoning extend to regulate individual conduct, constituting entrepreneurial subjects in an economic order.[28] For citizen-subjects of a liberal democracy under neoliberalism, citizenship and political activeness do not mean just acknowledging one's responsibility for economic growth and self-governance, but also the active and voluntary involvement in the management of one's potential for social risks (for example, poverty, unemployment, and disempowerment).[29] In other words, this mode of governance or "bio-politics" of the population, in which marginalized people (such as the poor and "at-risk" youth) have become special objects of knowledge and targets of control, is amplified within a neoliberal regime that encourages self-responsibility and empowerment.

Drawing on Foucault's concept of governmentality as productive in making subjects, my phrasing of affirmative governmentality articulates the explicit set of rhetorics and practices aimed at affirming youth of color—not only as actors in their own lives, but also as community leaders—in their quest to become better democratic subjects. Specifically, I am concerned with youth organizing as a technology of affirmative governmentality exercised on youth of color at the site of nonprofit organizations. When youth organizing came into vogue among a select group of private foundations in the 1990s, it was posed as an ingenious strategy in providing potentially "at-risk" youth of color with community involvement opportunities that would lead not only to self-esteem and empowerment, but also to community responsibility. According to the Funders' Collaborative for Youth Organizing website, "Youth organizing is an innovative youth development and social justice strategy that trains young people in community organizing and advocacy, and assists them in employing these skills to alter power relations and create meaningful institutional change in their communities. Youth organizing relies on the power and leadership of youth acting on issues defined by and affecting young people and their communities, and involves them in the design, implementation, and evaluation of these efforts."[30] Supported by a handful of philanthropic foundations, practitioners, and advocates, many of whom helped form the Funders' Collaborative for Youth Organizing, nonprofit organizations set out to promote youth organizing as "new collective empowerment technique."[31] The key for many philanthropic investors is the potential of individual and collective transformation among marginalized youth. The collaborative claims: "We believe that those who are most affected by social inequities—poverty, lack of access to resources, structural and institutional racism—have deep knowledge of community issues, and when given the tools and resources to organize, can be highly effective in developing solutions."[32]

"Empowerment" operates here as a strategy of self-governance to make the powerless and politically apathetic act on their own behalf, but not necessarily to oppose the relations of power that made them powerless. In the words of Barbara Cruikshank, "Empowerment is a power relationship, a relationship of government."[33] This relationship of government operates through affirming and empowering traditionally marginalized populations, such as "at-risk" youth of color, allowing them to govern and improve themselves through their voluntary and active participation in community programs set up to help them. Specifically, this management of youth has involved—and continues to involve—intimate cooperation, not separation, among state representatives, private philanthropic foundations, and youth experts through community programs. Take, for instance, the passage of Oakland's Measure K, an amendment to the city charter that allocated city funds to after-school programs, mentioned at the beginning of this chapter. This was a unique city measure to increase public resources for social programs in a time of disinvestment in social services. But a closer look at Measure K reveals that its passage was heavily directed by the private sector through nonprofit organizations. The measure was incited largely by a report of the Urban Strategies Council, a community advocacy nonprofit organization, that described the persistent effects of poverty on Oakland's youngsters. The report's call for citywide policy changes and infrastructure support to promote healthy youth development was the boost needed to rally Oakland voters. The report was funded by private foundations, including the Evelyn and Walter Haas Jr. Fund, a prominent sponsor of youth organizing in the Bay Area, and modeled on an initiative in San Francisco brought about by a comparable partnership.[34]

In chapter 2, I elaborate on how similar collaborations produced the 1992 Carnegie Report that decisively influenced foundations' investment in nonprofit organizations for positive youth development and youth organizing. These ventures consider central nonprofit organizations to be the site on which the labor of youth prevention, intervention, and care is conducted. The report also illuminates the shift from a welfare to a neo-liberal state, in which responsibility for social services is increasingly transferred to nonprofit organizations. I show in this chapter that the belief in youth agency and empowerment stems from a shift in the field of youth services in the late 1980s from a "fixing" approach to one of promoting "positive youth development," in which youth are viewed as capable agents of empowerment.[35] It is a transformation that parallels the tenets of neoliberalism. But under neoliberalism, empowerment is not only a personal responsibility; it is also a community responsibility. Nikolas Rose refers to "re-figuring the territory of the government" as the "government through community."[36] This mutation to community governance foists state responsibilities onto individuals and their communities, who now are responsible for their own—and their community's—economic and social well-being.

The Nonprofitization of Activism and Race

The exercise of affirmative governmentality at the site of the nonprofit squarely situates youth of color organizing within the reach of state power. Likewise, social movements described as oppositional, such as the youth of color organizing movement, are not separate from the state proper, nor are they free of its economic rationales. An analysis of youth of color organizing must be tethered to the history of depoliticization of social movements waged by people of color and the nonprofitization of activism in the latter half of the twentieth century. In fact, approximately three-quarters of youth activist groups have nonprofit status, and with a few exceptions, they are "heavily foundation-dependent."[37] I am concerned, however, not only with state processes that limit social justice organizing but also the relations of power that enable civil society to act as a mode of affirmative governmentality. That is, we find in previous social justice movements the language of empowerment also informed the institutionalization of a framework for providing resources and opportunities to vulnerable and marginalized populations through the medium of nonprofit organizations. This went hand in hand with the promotion of self-governance as an affirmative mode of political governance.[38] Youth organizing follows rhetorics and strategies originating in the organizing efforts of the civil rights movement and subsequent ethnic power movements. Yet the onset of neoliberal philosophies and policies has dramatically affected the growth not only of ethnic nonprofit organizations, but also of activist-oriented nonprofits, which emerged simultaneously with and as a consequence of these social movements.

The processes named above drastically hinder the potential of nonprofit organizations and civil society more broadly to mobilize against state power. Civil society does not necessarily represent an alternative sphere for political activity, although such an assumption is commonly accepted. David Harvey explains: "The period in which the neoliberal state has become hegemonic has also been the period in which the concept of civil society—often cast as an entity in opposition to state power—has become central to the formulation of oppositional politics."[39] Yet civil society is central to the construction and maintenance of modern state power. Antonio Gramsci expands our understanding of state power to include the complex structure of civil society that serves the interests of the ruling class: "State = political society + civil society, in other words hegemony protected by the armour of coercion."[40] Stuart Hall elaborates on Gramsci's analysis: "The state is no longer conceived as simply an administrative and coercive apparatus—it is also 'educative and formative.' "[41] Power is exercised through this process of "civil hegemony." Hall explains: "What Gramsci is pointing to, here, is partly the diversification of social antagonisms, the 'dispersal' of power, which occurs in societies where hegemony is sustained, not exclusively through the enforced instrumentality of the state, but rather, it is grounded in the relations and institutions of civil society."[42]

Nonprofit organizations are one aspect of civil society and include a variety of institutions and associations, including hospitals, foundations, schools, museums, and grassroots organizations.[43] Nonprofits have a long history in the United States, but it was not until the late twentieth century that their numbers grew as a consequence of the organizing of the civil rights era, the steady dismantling of the welfare state and social service programs of the Great Society, and the government's increasing contracting of social services to nonprofit organizations. The activism of minority groups in the 1960s and 1970s underscored racial and class inequalities as central markers of subjectivization and identification, and activists demanded both equitable representation and the fair redistribution of economic resources. Their aim was to alleviate multiple axes of social inequality, such as racism, poverty, and political marginalization. Consequently, the 1960s saw changes in laws that explicitly prohibited racial discrimination as well as a boom in social welfare programs, which sought to specifically address racial minority groups' demands. Yet this trend must also be read as one of incorporation and a gradual neutralization of race and race-based political mobilization through the targeted affirmation and deployment of race as an empirical category of inquiry and intervention.[44] As a result, state efforts to address social inequality through moderate economic redistribution and limited political representation constitute what Nancy Fraser refers to as affirmative remedies, which do not address the underlying frameworks that generate such inequalities.[45]

In part, the state worked to separate race and racial identities from their political roots and turn them into a state category of incorporation and administration by transforming collective action against itself into the expansion of politically neutral nonprofit social services. Scholar-activists describe the role of the nonprofit sector in institutionalizing once radical oppositional groups in the United States as the "non-profit industrial complex."[46] Dylan Rodriguez defines it as "a set of symbiotic relationships that link political and financial technologies of state and owning class control with surveillance over public political ideology, including and especially emergent progressive and leftist social movements."[47] Factors that contributed to the co-optation of social justice movements into state establishments include the incorporation of these entities, lured through the promise of funds, into politically uncharged nonprofit social delivery organizations (such as mental health programs); the domestication of social problems and structural inequalities into the practice of administering social services to individuals and privatizing social problems, assisted by the professionalization of social work; and the legal regulation of political activity permissible for nonprofits under tax codes.[48] Further straining their effectiveness to implement structural changes, nonprofit organizations are compartmentalized and inhibited by funding streams that target specific programs (such as drug prevention programs for youth) as opposed to supporting core infrastructure and programming.[49]

Moreover, the cultural turn in racial politics toward an institutionalized multiculturalism, together with the promotion of race-neutral policies of cultural diversity that fail to address inequalities structured by race or other points of difference, poses serious challenges to race, identity, and politics today.[50] Chapter 3 grapples with the erasure of AYPAL participants as "youth of color" by other members of a multiracial coalition in their campaign to stop the expansion of juvenile hall, which was often described as a "black and brown" issue. I examine AYPAL's confrontation with institutionalized racial categories to unveil the role of the state and that of well-intentioned activists of color in mediating and managing racial projects. This chapter presents the ever more urgent need for communities of color to critique and rethink strategies and points of affiliations to build multiracial coalitions for political action. Both the establishment of race as a technology for the management of minoritized populations and the limitations of identity politics for creating coalitional possibilities require our close attention.

Furthermore, the devolution of the mid-twentieth century's moderate expansion of the welfare state increased the presence of nonprofit organizations to fill the void left by social services and programs of care once under the state's direction. But the state has not ceded all control of its services. Rather, it has embarked on a new relationship with the private sector by contracting social services out to nonprofit organizations. By the 1990s, government funds made up half, if not more, of the funding sources of nonprofit organizations that were traditionally financed by the private sector.[51] This contracting regime stresses the mutual dependence, not the autonomy, of state and civil society. Paralleling this transformation is the increasingly expansive role of private charity and philanthropic foundations in supporting nonprofit organizations.

Just as civil society is linked to the political state, it is also entrenched in its economic principles. In other words, nonprofits and their funders also follow capitalist logics. This means that, despite their not-for-profit status, the nonprofit sector and the philanthropic foundations in it are implicated in the expansion and development of capitalism and in mediating neoliberal governance both domestically and internationally. *Uncivil Youth* is in dialogue with a growing body of scholarship that carefully examines the role of nonprofit and nongovernmental organizations and their funders in mediating neoliberal governance and relationships of power.[52] I pay close attention to the challenges faced by youth organizers running nonprofits, who must write grants, possess business management skills, and be accountable to funders that emphasize market rationalities and measurable outcomes that often clash with social justice activists' sensibilities. One issue that AYPAL, like other youth organizing groups, struggled with was the need to address both individual youth development skills of self-esteem and self-confidence—along with the young people's educational improvement and leadership skills—and social justice outcomes, often referred to as the "youth development–youth organizing divide."[53] Also straining an overwhelming number of youth organizing nonprofits that depend on philanthropic foundations for their survival is the unreliability of these resources, which may follow specific funding topics and limit disbursement of general operating funds. Youth organizing nonprofits, unlike other traditional youth service programs (such as drug and violence prevention programs), rely less on public funds and more on the goodwill of charitable donations from foundations. The institutionalization of nonprofit organizations and their adherence to capitalist reasoning place them, and civil society at large, within the state's art of governance and power.

Youth and Politics

Although I am critical of the modes of modern governmentality and related powers exercised by the neoliberal state, I argue in this book that young people are not just subjects of governance. The book results from my initial attraction to AYPAL because its young people practiced bold and oppositional politics and also because the organization facilitated this activism. Political workshops on topics such as racism, sexism, colonialism, the prison-industrial complex, and Asian and Pacific Islander history and activism supported young people's structural analysis of power and inequalities. Workshops were also held on "community organizing 101"—identifying concrete demands, articulating targets for each demand, assessing organizational power, developing tactics and strategies, identifying allies and opponents, and producing campaign outlines—and these principles were put into practice as young people decided on and led community organizing campaigns. Respectively, the medium of youth of color organizing and the community programs that support it offer young people the tools and the language they need for political engagement. These political practices include both state-sponsored forms of democratic citizenship (generating active members of a polity) and oppositional politics (challenging state-enforced policies). But youth's activism is enabled and mobilized through the medium of nonprofit organizations, which have attachments to capital and state governance. These nonprofit organizations follow a tradition of youth management strategies to improve young people's life chances and enable them to become better and worthy individual citizen-subjects. In other words, voluntary participation in community programs (nonprofit or otherwise) is central to the construction of citizenship as a private practice of self-improvement. In the current moment, neoliberal policies of privatizing public resources and services have translated good citizenship and politics into practices of personal choice, consumption, charity, and volunteer service. Emphasis on citizenship and politics has shifted from the realm of social action (protest gatherings and meetings, contested public debates) to personal acts (voting, signing a petition, volunteering). By stressing collective action, youth organizing pushes against this individualizing focus, but it is not free from the logics of neoliberal governance of self-empowerment and community governance.

Youth organizing as social movement is indeed restrained by these relationships of power, but that does not mean that young people are not involved in political practices of opposition. Nor should civil society be overlooked as an important terrain of political struggle. Hall insightfully notes that Gramsci's expansive understanding of the state and its ties to civil society opens up new arenas and institutions in which to wage political struggle.[54] As I show in this book, the effects of neoliberal power are visible and palpable, and so are young people's challenges to these state efforts. However, at times this power is not easily identifiable or felt as oppressive. Instead, it can govern through affirmation and enlisting one's willing participation. It is in these occurrences and ruptures of power and resistance that I situate young people's activism and youth of color organizing as a vehicle for social change.

Politics, like power, is not static and uniform, but dynamic, multiple, and situated. Politics, I believe, includes a wide constellation of mediated social practices and social relationships that may reinforce and/or subvert relations of power. These practices of politics are individual and collective, as well as multifarious. The political practices of the young people I worked with included formal and informal practices of citizenship. The informal practices included the different forms of flexible citizenship that Sunaina Maira identified in her work on Muslim youth; these were not necessarily dissenting practices, but they were based on everyday practices of leisure, work, and popular culture.[55] Yet the political practices of the young people I examine in this book are weighted toward the collective and explicit expressions of oppositional politics. As participants in a youth activist organization with a clearly stated mission to promote social justice, AYPAL members, like their peers in similar youth organizing nonprofits, engaged in an analysis of social inequalities and oppositional collective action that challenged power (that of targeted individuals or of institutions). These efforts did result in concrete social change outcomes, such as when they stopped expansion of juvenile hall. But they were not always successful, as evidenced by the young people's failed attempts to repeal a federal immigration policy.

These political practices did not materialize solely as deeds; they were also expressed as sharp political critiques and analyses of state power and its policies. In chapters 3 and 4, I turn to the details and nuances made possible by ethnographic participant observations to illuminate how young people negotiated and responded to neoliberalism's powers, and how their activism points to creative and alternative possibilities for political work. Chapter 3 tells the story of how young people successfully fought against youth incarceration and directly challenged the state, which they identified as the source of their criminalization. Mobilizing under a collective political youth of color identity, they transformed youth crime from a problem of super-predatory "at-risk" youth of color (assumed to be male) into a social problem of state incarceration and criminalization. Youth of color redefined their involvement in nonprofit organizations as going beyond the mere practice of participating in programs to reduce their potential to commit crimes and delinquent acts by confronting the very powers that constructed and punished them as such "risky" subjects. I describe AYPAL youth learning about and questioning the deportation of Cambodian refugees under increased immigration controls in the US war on terror after September 11 in chapter 4. As part of their antideportation campaign, young people engaged in a number of practices that constitute the core of democratic participation, such as engaging with their congressional representative and holding public meetings and protests. But this process also made evident to AYPAL youth, especially because they were too young to vote, the limits of what constituted conventional political engagement in a representative democracy. Nonetheless, in their efforts to stop these deportations, young people challenged the discourses and practices of democratic citizenship and state reform to discipline the state's immigrant population and privatize "good citizenship" as an exercise of personal responsibility. They developed a sophisticated critique not only of neoliberal state structures for political participation, but also of the reach of US imperialism at home and abroad.

In this regard, young people's activism challenges and expands studies of youth political practices. First, the spirited and visible activism of the AYPAL members and others in the youth of color organizing movement dispute commonly accepted and widely disseminated representations of young people today as apathetic and apolitical. The social construction of youth and adolescence as a transitional phase obscures an examination of young people as active political subjects in their own right. Often an approach to youth and political participation is construed as something to be actualized not in the present but in the future, constructing young people as what Hava Gordon describes as "citizens in the making."[56] Such a construction also points to a recognition that young people's political agency—or lack thereof—is mediated by age inequalities and power structures.

Second, young people's political practices widen the research on youth political socialization from the usual focus on people's navigation of the formal realm of governmental policies, institutions, voting, and elected officials to a focus on youth participation in local neighborhood efforts for social change that challenge institutional power.[57] Understandings of civic engagement and civic participation now include more overt political involvement, some of which explicitly includes youth organizing activities.[58] As advocates of youth organizing note, youth activism broadens the spectrum of traditional youth development outcomes from a focus on the individual (such as building self-confidence, self-esteem, and a positive sense of identity) to include their engagement with society (such as sociopolitical awareness of social problems and belief in the power of youth to produce community change).[59] Moreover, community-based youth nonprofit organizations are important spaces in supporting positive youth development outcomes and political activism.[60] The attention now being paid to youth organizing and activism is extending the scope of research and literature on youth political participation, civic engagement, and positive youth development.

Third, young people's political participation and collective action resists trends to define political participation and citizenship as an individual practice, as opposed to a social practice. This is despite prominent state policies and private ventures intended to promote individual forms of volunteerism as a privileged form of citizenship among young people. Most notable is the launch of President George H. W. Bush's Thousand Points of Light program—later reinvigorated by his son, President George W. Bush—which promoted a concept of volunteerism and a vision of the United States as a network of charitable personal acts. Moreover, popular youth volunteer and service programs founded in the 1960s, such as Volunteers in Service to America (VISTA), that tackled social problems of poverty and other forms of inequality have increasingly shifted toward promoting individualized and marketable career skills, rendering volunteerism as individual deeds of goodwill rather than political practice. As a result of concentrated efforts and state programs to solicit youth volunteers, the volunteer rates for these programs steadily increased in the 1990s and continue to rise into the twenty-first century.[61] Youth are obviously not inactive per se; rather, their participation is reframed as personal service. Youth of color organizing, as I demonstrate, with its explicit collective challenge of social inequalities by targeting individuals and structures of power responsible for such disparities, distinguishes itself from such politically neutral trends of individual volunteerism.

Last, as politically active and democratically engaged actors, the young people I worked with did not correspond neatly to stereotypical images of youth of color as social problems or as the apolitical model minority. The Asian and Pacific Islander youth of AYPAL offers an alternative narrative of young people as political actors. The unprecedented waves of immigration after the passage of the Immigration and Nationality Act of 1965 inaugurated a new population boom in second-generation Asian American youth, as well as a proliferation of some excellent studies about them.[62] Missing from these studies, however, is attention to the political activism of second-generation youth and the formation of their political identities. Moreover, unlike many studies of second-generation Asian American youth, which tend to focus on middle-class (and/or upper-middle-class) college students or working professionals, in my research I worked with young people who were working-class high school students from immigrant and refugee families.[63] A reflection of Oakland's diverse demographic, my research into AYPAL included Southeast Asian (Cambodian, Laotian, and Mien) and Pacific Islander (Samoan and Tongan) youth, groups that have had relatively little visibility in Asian American studies.[64]

On Methods and AYPAL

My methodological approach attends to the means through which power relations shape and affirm young people as social and political actors, and also through which young people experience, negotiate, and contest these multiple vectors of power. The basis of this book began with my work as a volunteer and ethnographer of AYPAL over the course of three and a half years in the early 2000s. My introduction to the group came in fall 2000, when I worked on a community project with two of its staff members. In subsequent months I advocated for equitable educational policies and addressing the programming needs for Asian and Pacific Islander students and parents in Oakland. I learned more about AYPAL and its youth organizing activities, and I volunteered my services. My offer led to an introduction to and a series of conversations with the rest of the AYPAL staff, after which I quickly became integrated into the everyday practices and functioning of the group. Both the young people and adults came to accept and depend on me as a staff member and participant. I was introduced to others outside of AYPAL by my official title, "super volunteer."

I approached the field by attending to youth cultural production and the implications of young people's individual agency and collective forms of resistance.[65] In the course of this investigation, I also sought to grasp those articulations of power that contained young people's activism, which led me to interrogate the affirmative modes of governance and practices that may shape them as subjects, often without their awareness or consent. Although I rely first and foremost on my ethnography of and active involvement in AYPAL to tell this story, this book is not a traditional ethnography, nor does it rely solely on ethnographic methods.[66] Rather I draw on interdisciplinary methodologies to make my theoretical and political critique. In addition to my fieldwork, I utilize reports by youth practitioners (often produced in conjunction with private philanthropic foundations, policymakers, and scholars), organizational websites, and historical sources. I employ close readings of these sources and integrate the institutional histories of youth programs and policies to analyze the intersections of empowerment and criminalization of youth of color, the project of youth organizing, its nonprofit structures, and its attachments to neoliberal governmentality. In making use of these multiple forms of evidence, my work involves interdisciplinary methods found in cultural studies and social sciences. This methodological approach describes a humanistic social science or, to borrow from Clifford Geertz, a thick description that is an interpretive theory of culture.[67]

With this in mind, I nonetheless wish to elaborate on AYPAL and the time I spent with the group in order to situate this study in the larger context of Oakland and its Asian and Pacific Islander communities. Unlike the typical youth organizing group, AYPAL was a collective made up of youth participants from six different ethnic nonprofit organizations, or "sites," in Oakland. The six sites that constituted the collective during my fieldwork were Asian Community Mental Health Services, Filipinos for Affirmative Action, the Korean Community Center of the East Bay, the Lao Iu Mien Cultural Association, the Oakland Asian Student Educational Services, and the Pacific Islander Kie Association.[68] Each of the organizations came into being with their own histories and goals, and they can be categorized as general providers of direct services to specific ethnic clientele. For example, one of the groups, the Lao Iu Mien Culture Association, was formed in 1982 to provide social services such as translation services and programs to preserve their cultural heritage for Mien refugees from Laos's highlands. Moreover, each of these nonprofit organizations was established after the organizing push of the 1960s, in which new federal and state money became available for social programs directed at previously neglected Asian and Pacific Islander communities. In providing essential direct social services for the diverse groups that make up the Asian diaspora in Oakland today, the work of these organizations is not directly political. Embedded in this unique organizational structure, AYPAL is attached not only to the particular history of the nonprofit institutionalization of activism, but also to the political neutralization of race and identity.

Yet AYPAL was established with a deliberate political purpose. With the passage of Oakland's Measure K in 1996 that provided city funds for after-school programs, members of the Asian and Pacific Islander Youth Network, a group of community organizations serving Asian American youth in Oakland, discussed the need to create a youth activist component. Many community leaders involved in the network were also participants in the Asian American movement of the late 1960s or had been radicalized by it, and all of them believed that a political youth organizing group was missing among the direct service programs, which focused on tutoring and drug and violence prevention. Instead of creating a new nonprofit to fill this gap, an organizing structure emerged in which youth participants from the six named organizations came together to form AYPAL. The new group's focus would be to train young people in the principles of community organizing and promote youth leadership. Jason, one of the original staff members, recalled during an interview that the reason for this organizing structure was to keep AYPAL rooted in specific ethnic groups to have a community base from which to build youth leadership and activism.[69] This arrangement is what made sense for the group during the time I worked with it. (The organizing structure of AYPAL is different today than it was in the early 2000s.) In this book, I situate AYPAL within the larger context of the nonprofit institutionalization of activism and depoliticization of race. Similar to other nonprofit organizations that serve Asian and Pacific Islander populations, AYPAL and its affiliate organizations fulfill multiple purposes, including (but not limited to) providing direct services, mobilizing its members for political action in response to state-sponsored disparities, and facilitating the cultural incorporation and assimilation of its participants into the US body politic.[70]

The six ethnic nonprofit organizations that made up AYPAL also reflected the larger community profile of Asian and Pacific Islanders, which was remarkably different in the early 2000s than in the late 1960s. The 1965 Immigration and Nationality Act, passed in a period of civil rights legislation, lifted a century's worth of restrictive exclusion laws and quotas for immigration from Asian countries, allowing new immigrants to enter the United States who diversified the race, class, and gender composition of the existing Asian American population. Paul Ong and John Liu note: "After 1965, Asia became a major source of immigration . . . constituting less than 4 percent of total U.S. immigration between 1921 and 1960 and 42 percent from 1981 to 1989."[71] The influx of these new immigrants transformed the Asian American community from a largely native-born population to a chiefly foreign-born one. Moreover, the family reunification preferences of the 1965 law changed what had been primarily "bachelor societies," evening out their gender imbalances. The law's employment preferences selectively recruited highly educated experts such as engineers, scientists, doctors, and nurses, so that the population shifted to heavily represent middle-class professionals. The US involvement in the wars in Southeast Asia resulted in the arrival of political refugees from Cambodia, Laos, and Vietnam, groups that were not represented in significant numbers until the late 1970s.

Oakland absorbed all these changes. The city in the 1970s was home to waves of new Asian immigrants and refugees from Cambodia, China, Hong Kong, Korea, Laos, Taiwan, and Vietnam, as well as ethnic Chinese displaced from Southeast Asia.[72] According to the 2000 US Census, the

Asian and Pacific Islander community overall made up 15.8 percent of Oakland's population, representing diverse ethnic groups. The Chinese, often descended from earlier Chinese settlers in the United States, composed the largest group, followed by the Vietnamese, Filipinos, Cambodians, Laotians, Japanese, Koreans, Asian Indians, and Tongans.[73] These histories critically inform the constitution of AYPAL, in terms of both its demographics and its political concerns.

The core of AYPAL was a group of youth interns and adult staff members. Each of the six AYPAL groups hired approximately seven to ten interns every summer; comprising a core group of up to sixty total participants.[74] The majority, but not all, came from working-class families and lived in Oakland's ethnic enclaves, where they attended the city's public schools. Each site operated independently on a day-to-day basis, but they also worked together as a cohesive group. An AYPAL adult staff member, or "site coordinator," led each of the six groups. In their specific groups, interns met three times a week. One of the major tasks that each of the specific ethnic groups was responsible for was to run weekly Youth Leadership Organizations meetings. The interns were responsible for recruiting their peers for the meetings, and planning and facilitating them. Consisting of workshops on subjects ranging from "elements of hip-hop" to gentrification, the meetings allowed a larger pool of young people who were not paid interns to participate in AYPAL activities. Attendance varied by site, ranging from twenty to eighty young people at any one of the meetings. Held throughout Oakland neighborhoods—such as in the San Antonio–Fruitvale area for Mien and Cambodian youth, in Chinatown for Chinese and Vietnamese youth, and in East Oakland for Pacific Islander youth—these Youth Leadership Organizations meetings reflected the diversity of the Asian and Pacific Islander community of Oakland and the ethnic nonprofit organizations that had formed to meet their needs. Uniting these different groups were the political workshops, community organizing campaign work, and a cultural arts program. The six AYPAL groups met at least once a month, if not more often, for these all-site "Jedi" meetings. Other joint meetings included political or social activities such as rallies, marches, and special trips.

My ethnography consisted of participation in and participant-observation of a wide constellation of AYPAL organizational activities. On any given week, I spent at least four out of five weekdays at its meetings and one and sometimes both weekend days at AYPAL-related events. I attended and led daily youth meetings; prepped youth for Youth Leadership Organizations meetings; spent late nights and early mornings with other adult staff members planning workshops; facilitated workshops; sat in on weekly staff meetings; joined the group's members at political rallies, protests, and community forums; made school visits to young people in the program; and participated in various AYPAL social occasions, such as dinners, movies, and camping trips. I took copious field notes at all AYPAL activities and events. I conducted in-depth, semistructured, one-on-one interviews with eighteen youth and eight adult staff members (the interviews were approximately one to one-and-a-half hours in length and were tape-recorded and transcribed). I also conducted nine youth focus group interviews, involving approximately seventy young people in all. In sum, over three and a half years, I came into contact with a large number of people who participated in AYPAL activities. I developed close ties with many of them. In this manner, my time in the field was a politically engaged activist ethnography, as I was simultaneously engaged in research for social critique and in political action.[75]

Chapter 1

CIVILIZING YOUTH AGAINST DELINQUENCY

Community-based programs have been and continue to be an important youth intervention strategy to enable technologies of affirmative governmentality. In recent decades, a host of private and public actors—foundations, companies, state agencies, and nonprofit organizations—have organized to meet young people's specific needs. The services provided are direct (educational tutoring, mental and sexual health services), rehabilitative (drugs, mental illness), and preventive (drugs, violence, pregnancy, risky sexual behavior); promote positive youth development (self-confidence, teamwork, leadership skills); and involve youth activism. In this chapter, I situate the youth organizing movement and the emergence of these agencies and actors in the 1990s within a historical context going back to the late nineteenth century, in which programs were created to transform poor, marginalized, immigrant, and ethnic youth to become better democratic subjects. In the Progressive Era, youth or adolescence was established as a social category of inquiry and intervention and as a subject of state regulation, a schema that continues to shape young people's lives in the current moment. Progressive Era reformers inaugurated a wide variety of community institutions and programs targeted exclusively at young people that took the form of after-school programs, industrial and vocational schools, settlement houses, and reformatories. Not coincidentally, the first US juvenile court was created in 1899 in Illinois by social reformers as an advance in child welfare to refine "delinquent" youth.[1] The fact that these institutions were founded in the same period, I argue, reveals something crucial about the emergence of youth as a category of governance in the current moment.

Those who wanted to make youth into better democratic subjects in the late nineteenth century did not acknowledge a sense of individual youth agency like the one we see as part of affirmative governmentality today. Nor did speaking of a youth delinquent then connote images of the super-predator young criminal of color as it does today. But these early youth intervention institutions and strategies of social control did set a precedent found in current relations of power to care and to govern. Moreover, like today, strategies of youth care and control were related to categories of class, race, and gender and involved interrelationships between state and civil society. I touch on youth intervention strategies of the late nineteenth and early twentieth century not to produce a historical account, but rather to show that current youth organizing and activist programs are the latest permutation of youth improvement techniques that represent linked strategies of social control to empower and to criminalize.

Youth and Adolescence:
A Special Category of Social Care and Control

The subjugation of young people as a powerless group in need of improvement (as in community-based youth programs) or punishment (as in the juvenile justice system), as well as a subjective population capable of reform and self-empowerment, depends on the creation and manageability of young people as a problematic category of inquiry and a target of intervention. Social investments in enabling and controlling young people can be traced to the late nineteenth century and the early twentieth, particularly to institutional and ideological movements in the Progressive Era and the "benevolent" social reform efforts by its "child-savers"—"an amalgam of philanthropists, middle-class reformers and professionals."[2] This was a period of tremendous social change in the United States. As Anthony Platt notes, the child-saving movement "reflected massive changes in the mode of production, from laissez-faire to monopoly capitalism, and in strategies of social control, from inefficient repression to welfare state benevolence."[3] Rapid capitalist expansion and the shift in labor from agriculture to urban factories accompanied migration to the cities, especially among young women; and increasing immigration widened social inequality and heightened social turmoil. Faced with growing social concerns over crime, disease, and social deterioration, as well as social unrest resulting from these conditions, Progressive Era reformers needed to ameliorate the poor living conditions of less-privileged, city-dwelling counterparts. Also of social concern were the immigrants newly arrived from Southern, Eastern, and Central Europe who were not quite considered white (such as Greek, Irish, Italian, and Jewish immigrants).[4] In a period of increased immigration (thirteen million new European immigrants arrived between 1886 and 1925), Asian exclusion laws, and legal challenges to race-based citizenship, social reformers ameliorated social anxieties about race and racial and class inequality by targeting their efforts at rescuing a select group of European immigrants—still-developing children and youth—deemed worthy of rescue. Progressive Era reformers, businessmen, cultural elites, and politicians alike were particularly distressed by the vices and "degeneracy" of these poor urban dwellers.[5]

Thus, young people became a special category of concern serving as important metaphors for reshaping a society in transition. Attempts to regulate young people relied on emerging notions of science and medical knowledge to categorize, identify, diagnose, and treat certain subjects. Developments in the social and life sciences that focused on adolescence as a topic of inquiry and object of research converged to cement adolescence as a distinct life stage in need of intervention and social control. In 1904 the psychologist G. Stanley Hall published his very influential *Adolescence: Its Psychology and Its Relations to Physiology, Anthropology, Sociology, Sex, Crime, and Religion.*[6] The book characterized adolescence as a distinct physical and psychological stage of storm and stress and described young people as experiencing hormonal and emotional turmoil, a portrayal that is now commonly accepted. Hall presented parallels between human development and human evolution, naturalizing adolescence as a discrete phase characterized by traits that are biological (physical and hormonal changes), psychological (emotional instability, irresponsibility, frivolous behavior), and social (rebellion, orientation toward peers). Hall also standardized "normal" adolescent development and the adolescent as a white, heterosexual, middle-class male against which non-normative young people could be judged—and then treated in social programs.[7] Youth intervention approaches are often based on such deeply naturalized biological assumptions, through which the impetus to protect young people presumes their innocence and immaturity, while discourses to regulate them depend on widespread beliefs of their uncontrollable hormones and emotions. What is significant about this categorization of young people as an object of knowledge is their social construction as subjects of governance and intervention. Barbara Cruikshank writes: "For social programs to be territorialized, they must be known. For government to solve the 'social problems' of poverty, delinquency, dependency, crime, self-esteem, and so on, it must have a certain kind of knowledge that is measurable, specific, and calculable, knowledge that can be organized into governmental solutions. Social scientific knowledge is central to the government of the poor, to the very formation of the poor as an identifiable group."[8]

The period in which young people became legitimate objects of scientific inquiry and knowledge also coincided with the creation of social programs and institutions that segregated young people into age-specific spaces for intervention. Establishment of new institutions and programs affirmed that young people were fundamentally different from adults and were special subjects in need of adult care and control. The phasing out of child labor and state enactment of school attendance laws expanded educational institutions and services. Social and community programs were established to deal with young people outside schools, in both informal and formal groups found at settlement houses, after-school programs, public parks and recreation facilities, and private industrial and vocational schools. Juvenile courts and affiliated correctional centers—including halfway houses, shelters, camps, maternity homes, and reformatories—were also instituted at this time. These various social programs for young people were based on numerous rationales and provided a wide range of services, but they had in common the role of reforming and training poor, immigrant, and marginalized young people to become better citizen-subjects. In his historical study of after-school programs, Robert Halpern observes: "Progressive reformers began reinterpreting the 'problem' of working-class children's out-of-school time as an opportunity, to use that time to improve those children, and through that effort ultimately to improve society."[9] The management of young people was based on biological and psychological assumptions of their vulnerability and uncontrollability, and these intervention programs were posed as an opportunity to protect young men and women from the risks of crime, poverty, and other social ills. In tackling issues stemming from the perceived negligence and inadequacy of immigrant parents, the vices and dangers of the city streets, and female sexual immorality, youth intervention programs reflected social concerns and tensions over race, class, and gender that were shrouded by the premise of benevolence and reform.

Philanthropy, Reformers, and
Community Programs of Care and Reform

Jane Addams, the most widely recognized and celebrated reformer of the Progressive Era and, with Ellen Starr, cofounder of the Hull House settlement in 1889, best exemplified the progressive tradition of reform and social control. For Addams and her fellow child-savers, youth were in need of control and it was the reformers' responsibility to care for them; neglecting to provide youth with wholesome activities would lead to delinquency and other unproductive behavior. As Addams wrote in her widely read *The Spirit of Youth and the City Streets*, first published in 1909: "To fail to provide for the recreation of youth, is not only to deprive all of them of their natural form of expression, but is certain to subject some of them to the overwhelming temptation of illicit and soul-destroying pleasures."[10] One of the earliest activities that Addams and Starr offered at the Hull House were clubs and classes to expose their less fortunate residents to fine arts and literature: "One of their primary tasks, they believed, was to bring an appreciation of beauty and great art to those forced to live in the drab and unattractive slums."[11] These clubs and classes were soon joined by a kindergarten, homemakers' clubs, cooperative residence for working girls, music school, sewing and book clubs, and many other activities. The Hull House instigated what became a national movement—by 1911 there were more than four hundred social settlements across the country.[12]

In addition to settlement houses, other social agencies provided activities including after-school programs, industrial training classes, church programs, and clubs. For instance, after-school programs were first started as small "boys clubs" that in part grew out of the limits of settlement houses to provide for "boys' work," as these places were viewed as more suited for girls.[13] These after-school programs had a variety of sponsoring agencies, including churches, YMCAs, municipal departments of parks and recreations, libraries, and some schools. An example was the North Bennet Street Industrial School, "a charitable institution dedicated to providing social services, industrial and vocational training, and Americanization programs to immigrants in the North End of Boston."[14]

In 1899, as noted previously, the first US juvenile court was created in Illinois, across the street from the Hull House in Chicago and in close connection with its reformers. A fundamental rationalization for a juvenile court system was the need to rescue children from existing jails and separate them from criminal adult offenders.[15] The juvenile justice court was based on the premise of the British doctrine of *parens patriae*, the state as parent and as an agent of care. Platt writes that the Chicago Bar Association viewed the 1899 Illinois juvenile court act as follows: "that the State, acting through the Juvenile Court, exercises that tender solicitude and care over its neglected, dependent wards that a wise and loving parent would exercise with reference to his own children under similar circumstances."[16] This premise also holds that the state has the right and responsibility (and power) to intervene in the welfare of the dependent, neglected, or delinquent child: "The courts could also commit [to an institution] children who were found to be 'destitute of proper parental care, or growing up in mendicancy, ignorance, idleness or vice.'"[17] Entrenched in a discourse of rehabilitation, the dominant prescription was therapy, not punishment. The titles given to individual actors who worked with young people is a case in point: court judges were referred to as "doctor-counselors"; lawyers were "therapists"; and prison (detention) guards were "reform doctors."[18] Supporters of the Hull House served as the first probation officer of the juvenile court (Alzina Stevens) and chairwomen of the Juvenile Court Committee (Julia Lathrop and Louise Bowen).[19] Touted as a system of reform and rehabilitation, the "child-savers hoped to demonstrate that delinquents were capable of being converted into law-abiding citizens."[20] The most highly regarded form of youth rehabilitation was the reformatory, where city youth were sent to an institution in the country to be separated from the vices of urban life and their unfit parents for an indeterminate period of healthy treatment, found in a rural life and agricultural labor.

Social and community programs, including juvenile court, were largely established by the charitable donations of wealthy philanthropists who were members of the cultural and political elite. For instance, the North Bennet Street Industrial School was established in 1880 by Pauline Agassiz Shaw, the daughter of an affluent family, and was put under the direction of the Associated Charities of Boston, a philanthropic organization serving the needs of immigrants in Boston's North End. The Hull House was supported by a distinguished list of prosperous patrons, many who were prominent society women who donated time and money to the settlement house.[21] The bulk of people who carried out youth reform were women, many of them wives and daughters of the industrial gentry. Well educated and well traveled, they came from privileged social and political backgrounds.[22] Addams was the scion of a wealthy family, and her father was a Republican senator in the Illinois legislature. She was the first woman to receive a bachelor's degree from Rockford Female Seminary (renamed Rockford College), where she met Ellen Starr—the cofounder of the Hull House. When faced with changing domestic roles wrought by separation of home and work, these women found a niche in philanthropy—either as traditional benefactresses of society or as career women rescuing and saving children and youth.[23] The very forces that created social anxiety over their poorer counterparts enabled these women to take on more prominent social roles. Becoming frontline workers in newly established youth intervention programs, they were teachers, social workers, juvenile court wardens and officers, and police officers, and they ran reformatories.[24] Through such roles, these middle-class women attained new social and professional status: it was generally believed that child-saving work was more suited for women than men, based on women's ability to nurture and care—especially in dealing with delinquents.[25]

Ironically, in their new professional roles, these women enforced traditional ideals of gender, home, and family, turning their attention to immigrant youth and the perceived inadequacy of their recently arrived parents. Halpern writes that after-school "sponsors commonly cited family neglect and inadequacy as a rationale for their work. Immigrant parents were deemed incapable of preparing their children for the demands of a complex, industrial society; and their values were deemed irrelevant, even harmful, to their children."[26] The project of Americanization and assimilation was central to these social and community programs. At the Hull House there was "basic instruction in English language and American government to aid the immigrant who was desperately trying to learn new American ways."[27] Kate Larson observes of the North Bennet Street Industrial School that "it was through the multitude of literary, debate, and athletic clubs for boys and young men, and sewing, cooking, and a few literary clubs for girls and young women that reformers and immigrants often experienced their first cross-class and cross-cultural exchanges."[28] The hope was that by directly exposing immigrant children to upper-middle-class, well-educated volunteers and social reformers, the latter's values and decorum could be learned by and transferred to the former. Furthermore, such exposure would civilize others: "The goal here was both to change the children's own values and behavior and to use children to change the values and behavior of their parents, as new practices were brought home."[29]

Community Programs against
Delinquency and Sexual Immorality

Although social and community programs were promoted as a means of reforming children and youth to become better citizens, the programs were also a medium of social control. Young people were the subjects that came to be the focus of social anxieties over urbanization, increasing social inequality, crime, and changing sexual norms. Like other reformers, Addams saw social and community programs, including juvenile justice, as an opportunity to provide proper guidance of young people's unfettered time and deter them from juvenile delinquency and crime. Moreover, it was believed that young people's propensity for such risks and risky behavior was based on their innate immaturity and volatility, a belief informed by prevailing conceptions of adolescence as a distinct stage of life that needed proper care and control. In a review of material collected from juvenile courts by participants at the Hull House, Addams asserted: "The young people are overborne by their own undirected and misguided energies. A mere temperamental outbreak in a brief period of obstreperousness exposes a promising boy to arrest and imprisonment, an accidental combination of circumstances too complicated and overwhelming to be coped with by an immature mind, condemns a growing lad to a criminal career."[30]

Specifically, social and community programs were posed as an alternative to the crime and vices of the urban street life. Addams declared: "This period of life is difficult everywhere, but it seems at times as if a great city almost deliberately increased its perils. The newly awakened senses are appealed to by all that is gaudy and sensual, by the flippant street music, the highly colored theater posters, the trashy love stories, the feathered hats, the cheap heroics of the revolvers displayed in the pawn-shop windows. This fundamental susceptibility is thus evoked without a corresponding stir of the higher imagination, and the result is as dangerous as possible."[31] She decried theaters, saloons, and dance halls as inappropriate venues where young people went to quench their desires for adventure and to relieve the loneliness of city life and the monotony of factory work. Instead, her solution was to provide more wholesome opportunities and play activities such as arts, sports, and chaperoned dances at parks and recreational halls. Addams argued that programs were needed to properly harness youth's "primitive instincts," including a "desire for pleasure" and "sexual susceptibility."[32]

Indeed, of particular concern to women reformers was the sexual morality or "sexual susceptibility" of their less-fortunate and less-educated counterparts, particularly young and unmarried women. Fears over sexual immorality reflected social anxieties over these women's social and sexual autonomy, newly enabled by urban employment and leisure. This period brought an unprecedented number of single women from poor, working-class families to the cities for employment: "By the end of the 19th century, young women aged 15 to 24 made up over a third of the adult female population, a record high proportion; furthermore, 72% of these women were unmarried. . . . The disproportionately high rate of young, single women in cities who were seeking work, roughly one third of whom were living on their own without their parents' supervision, prompted fears of immorality, danger, and societal degeneration."[33] Their pronounced special status and sheer visibility in the city streets increased the attention they attracted. In her work on such "delinquent daughters," Mary Odem comments: "As they challenged traditional roles and expectations, working-class daughters became the focus of great social anxiety. Their move outside the home was linked to a host of social problems—prostitution and vice, venereal disease, family breakdown, and out-of-wedlock pregnancy."[34] The political and cultural elite upheld Victorian codes of "civilized morality," in which "any sexual activity outside the bonds of wedlock was simultaneously a cause and a symbol of moral degradation."[35] Moreover, the elites believed that "upon adherence to the code of civilized morality rested not just the welfare of individuals, but of the entire society."[36]

Deemed the population most at risk of breaching the code of sexual morality, young unmarried women became special targets of social interventions that were different from those directed at their male peers. Unlike young men, who were targeted for their idleness or vagrancy, young women were stigmatized by their potential sexual behavior. Places of work—offices, stores, and factories—like places of entertainment—theaters, dance halls, and amusement parks—were all possible places for committing sexual indiscretions, prompting the need for surveillance and the prevention of such behaviors. Social and community programs provided by settlements like the Hull House or other charitable associations hence were posed as a direct alternative, designed to prevent young unmarried women's sexual immorality. Larson describes the young women's literary club that was started at the North Bennet Street Industrial School this way:

Burdened by the directive to "draw these girls in, from the perils of the street"
... [the director] sought to organize the clubs along the same lines as the more
literary and educational clubs that already existed for boys. These "perils" were
a constant theme throughout the reform literature of the time period. Saloons, dance halls, and other "cheap" amusements were thought of as precur-
sors to prostitution and the loss of morality. While the threat of prostitution
and entrapment in white slavery was real for some vulnerable, single, poor,
and immigrant women, middle-class observers' uneasiness with the explicit
or potential sexuality of these young women created a tension that manifested
itself as an assumption that all poor, immigrant women needed to be morally
and physically protected. In fact, many young immigrant women were also
concerned with projecting an image of middle-class respectability and "social
purity." The reality was that most Jewish and Italian parents would not allow
their daughters out of the house in the evening without a chaperon, usually an
older sibling (preferably male) or other relative.[37]

Although as we can see that attempts to control these young women were
of central concern to their parents as well, these parents were often deemed
inadequate by social reformers, and the regulation of their children's sexuality became a social concern and problem.

We find in the Progressive Era that social and community programs directed at young people were alternatives to an otherwise inevitable progress
along the path of juvenile delinquency and sexual corruption—caused by
inadequate and negative family environments, the vices and potential criminality of the streets, and sexual immorality of young unmarried women—
and thus offered a solution to a host of social problems. The link between
strategies to reform and control youth is clearly laid out in this period, as
shown in the programs established on their behalf.

Juvenile Courts and the
Institutionalization of Youth Delinquency

Like courses in comportment and literature, the juvenile court was instituted following the principles of care and governance. At the same time, the
court was different in its targeting of youth as state subjects of regulation.
The institutionalization of the juvenile court system since the Progressive
Era has cemented into law the definition of youth delinquency. The system

constructed youth delinquency not only as a distinct social category of analysis and intervention, but also as a legal category that continues today. Platt documents how, in the creation of a separate juvenile court system, the child-savers "brought attention to—and, in doing so, invented—new categories of youthful misbehavior which were hitherto unappreciated."[38] This enabled courts to investigate a wide variety of youth practices and behaviors as "delinquent," which in the earlier part of the nineteenth century had not been regarded as such or placed under government law and control. Platt explains: "Statutory definitions of 'delinquency' included (1) acts that would be criminal if committed by adults, (2) acts that violated county, town or municipal ordinances, and (3) violations of vaguely defined catchalls—such as 'vicious or immoral behavior,' 'incorrigibility,' 'truancy,' 'profane or indecent language,' 'growing up in idleness,' 'living with any vicious or disreputable person,' etc.—which indicated, if unchecked, the possibility of more serious misconduct in the future."[39] The Illinois juvenile court act of 1899 also authorized the penalization of pre-delinquent behavior. Through such measures, these delinquent behaviors or status offenses—offenses committed only by juveniles—might be corrected and these young people reformed to become better citizen-subjects.

Furthermore, this institutionalization of delinquency and its consequences were mapped differently for young women and men. The most common offenses for young men were acts against property or persons. Addams provides in her book a list of charges that boys incurred in juvenile courts, including "throwing stones at moving train windows," "stealing a horse blanket to use at night when it was cold sleeping on the wharf," "calling a neighbor a 'scab,'" and "resisting an officer."[40] These offenses are described and viewed by Addams as innocuous, with the boys compelled to perform such acts by their "desire for adventure" underscoring the "spirit of the youth." For young women, however, the definition of delinquency was quite different: "The term 'delinquency,' as applied to females in the early years of the twentieth century, *meant* overt sexuality. . . . During the nineteenth and for much of the twentieth century, offenses against sexual morality, a rubric that covered a wide range of behaviors from staying out late at night to pregnancy, were the principal reasons for which unmarried young women were prosecuted in court and committed to reformatories."[41] The majority of young women brought before juvenile courts were charged with "immorality"—a catchall term that usually indicated the likelihood that sexual intercourse had taken place—waywardness, and/or incorrigibility, which overwhelmingly referred to sexual misconduct.[42] Evidence of such offenses was sought by questioning these young women or their suspected male partners or neighbors, and it was supported by surveillance reports of their leisure activities and gynecological exams. Other status offenses common to women included running away and disobedience to parents.[43]

The juvenile court presented itself as a "benevolent yet stern father" that admonished and penalized the wayward girl in the hope of making her become a better citizen.[44] In accordance to Victorian notions of women's sexuality as chaste and passive, the "delinquent girl" was viewed as innocent and her promiscuity was perceived as redeemable. Preference for placement in intervention programs was given to younger women (as they were still deemed young and innocent enough to change), girls pregnant for the first time, and those without venereal diseases.[45] Men were considered responsible in sexual immorality cases, as evidenced by the use of statutory rape charges against them and movements to raise the age of consent in state laws across the United States. Efforts to abolish white slavery were also first premised on young women's innocence. Changing sexual practices soon challenged this focus on chaste young females in need of protection. Constance Nathanson notes that by the early 1920s, "sex, as well as work, before marriage became redefined as valuable preliminaries to a lifetime career of domestic bliss. Sexual experimentation (within limits) was legitimized as preparation for marriage, intercourse was sanctified by engagement, and paid work became a means to accelerate the day of the wedding."[46] Additionally, sex was consensual in three-quarters of the statutory rape cases brought in Los Angeles courts in this period.[47]

Regardless, the punishment of young women's delinquency, or the costs of their sexual immorality, was more severe than for young men: "For example, the Chicago family court sent half the girl delinquents but only a fifth of the boy delinquents to reformatories between 1899 and 1909. In Milwaukee, twice as many girls as boys were committed to training schools. . . . In Honolulu . . . girls were twice as likely as males to be detained for their offenses and, on average, spent five times as long in detention as their male counterparts. They were also nearly three times more likely to be sentenced to the training school."[48] The double standard of this "judicial paternalism" that applies youth delinquency to the sexual mores of young

women and not to those of young men continues to have unequal consequences. Since the invention of juvenile delinquency, young women continue to be overrepresented in status offenses (such as running away and
incorrigibility) and are more likely to be arrested for their alleged sexual
misbehavior.[49]

Although shrouded in a discourse of benevolence as a technology of citizenship, the juvenile court system from its inception has been a form of
social control to regulate delinquent poor, marginalized, ethnic, and immigrant young boys and girls, shaping them into law-abiding citizens. In reality, many of the institutions to which young people were sentenced were not
free of abuse or violence. As Platt reveals, military officers often carried out
discipline in reformatories that involved whippings, confinement, and
young people being handcuffed to pipes for days, to name a few punishments. He adds: "Some boys were punished by being locked up in the 'hole'
for up to thirty-two days with no shoes and no mattress. They slept on
wooden boards nailed to the concrete floor. Some were handcuffed to iron
pipes and kept manacled day and night."[50] Platt argues that the creation of
the juvenile justice system was a way to develop and legitimate a new state
and capitalist class, a technique of corporate elite and state expansion to
maintain cultural hegemony: "The child saving movement tried to do for
the criminal system what industrial capitalists and corporate leaders were
trying to do for the economy—that is, achieve order, stability and control
while preserving the existing class system and distribution of wealth."[51]
Young people came to represent special subjects of inquiry and intervention
in a period of tremendous social, political, economic, and demographic up-
heaval; widening social inequality; and changing gender and sexual norms.
Underlying the institutionalization of the juvenile court was the assumption
that these youth were subjects in need of care and control, reflecting the
hegemonic powers of capitalism and liberal state governance.

We find in this historical perspective that the establishment of social
programs for youth—specifically juvenile courts and community programs
—by Progressive Era reformers institutionalized youth intervention strategies of social control premised on improving young people so they could
become better future citizens. These premises still hold today. Although
typical conceptions and legal definitions of youth delinquency in this earlier era were (in Platt's words) "growing up in mendicancy, ignorance,
idleness or vice" as opposed to the common representations today of vio-

lent "super-predator" young criminals, what remains are the close links between intervention strategies to reform (and enable) young men and women and programs to prevent (and control) them from becoming "risky," uncivil subjects, sexually or otherwise.[52]

The Current Tradition:
Criminalizing Uncivil Youth of Color

The juvenile justice system today no longer resembles the system established by reformers of the Progressive Era to rehabilitate poor, immigrant, working-class, delinquent young people to become better citizen-subjects; rather, it is one of punishment and overt social control. Starting in the 1980s, the "pendulum began to swing to law and order."[53] Ruth Wilson Gilmore notes that "crime" more generally, not just youth crime, was treated differently, both objectively and subjectively from the 1980s onward. For instance, in California, the state has initiated up to 200 new pieces of legislation since 1988 in a "criminal-law production frenzy" that introduced a host of new criminalization and punishment tactics—such as enhanced prison sentences, new crimes, and the "three strikes law"—and targeted drugs and gangs that disproportionately affected poor, racial minority populations.[54] At the end of the twentieth century, fears of youth crime figured centrally in a national effort by politicians and voters to get tough on crime and take drastic measures against inner-city crime, gangs, and violence, producing an unprecedented crackdown on juvenile crime.[55] Gilmore continues: "Politicians of all races and ethnicities merged gang membership, drug use, and habitual criminal activity into a single social scourge, which was then used to explain everything from unruly youth to inner-city homicides to the need for more prisons to isolate wrongdoers."[56] Beyond juvenile justice, young people bore the burden of curfews, increased surveillance measures and police enforcement in schools, and anti-gang laws to control their behavior.[57] Paralleling this retribution against youth—in particular, youth of color—was the rise of youth intervention programs aimed at caring for and "fixing" young people (white and non-white), saving them from drugs, violence, and crime.[58]

The trend toward overt punishment and youth incarceration is paradoxically linked to the expansion of youth rights. A series of US Supreme Court cases starting in the late 1960s marked the legal shift of juvenile justice from a system of reform to a system of criminal courts for youth offenders.[59] In particular, in the 1967 case *In re Gault*, the court rejected the doctrine of *parens patriae* that gave the state the power and responsibility to protect young people on the basis of their immature physical and cognitive capabilities. The court ruled that young people, like their adult counterparts, are fully responsible and hence also in need of full constitutional protection. The *Gault* case, along with others in this period, extended to young people basic constitutional rights such as due process, the right to counsel, and the right to question witnesses.[60] In doing so, it expanded young people's rights in the form of legal procedural safeguards. But it also legitimized the imposition of more punitive consequences, such as the ability to try and sentence young people as adults and incarcerate them with adults—which, ironically, was the impetus for early social reformers to create a separate system for juveniles. Although the 1974 Federal Juvenile Delinquency Act sought to deinstitutionalize status offenses and divert those convicted of minor youth offenses (such as violating liquor laws) to outside agencies, deinstitutionalize young people already in the criminal justice system, and separate youth from adult offenders, such safeguards were amended with "get tough on crime" measures in the 1980s and 1990s, which once again allowed juveniles to be tried as adults for some violent crimes and weapons violations and reorganized the juvenile justice system to resemble an adult criminal justice system.

Youth of color, particularly African American and Latino males, are both the targets and victims of these changes. Measures to prevent and stop youth violence stemmed from perceptions of an uncontrollable rise in the numbers of crimes committed by dangerous youth of color roaming the streets. John DiIulio, a political science professor, warned of "war stories about the ever-growing numbers of hardened, remorseless juveniles who were showing up in the system" and "super-predatory" young men committing homicidal violence in "wolf packs."[61] DiIulio played on mainstream fears of dangerous young men of color who needed to be sharply controlled. His image of the super-predator captures in a nutshell mainstream anxieties and assumptions, as well as the prominent appearances of African American and Latino male youth in the popular media as perpetrators of crime and youth delinquency.[62]

Despite fears of a new generation of dangerous super-predators on the loose, such alarms were unfounded. Between 1975 and 1997, California's teenage population increased by half a million; but 80,000 fewer teenagers were arrested in the mid-1990s than in the mid-1970s.[63] Drawing on Federal Bureau of Investigation data, Barry Feld reports: "While serious and violent crimes capture media and public attention, police arrested three-quarters (75 percent) of all juveniles for nonindex and status offenses."[64] In other words, the majority of young people arrested today, as in earlier decades, are charged with status offenses (such as truancy, running away, curfew violation, the possession and consumption of alcohol, and the purchase of cigarettes). The images of the super-predator and the violent youth of color criminal do not match the reality of the typical juvenile delinquent. Additionally, although the rates of youth crime and crime in general peaked in the 1980s, they have declined steadily since then.[65] As Mike Males observes, "*For 20 years, crime trends have been dramatically and diametrically the opposite of what California officials and the media have been saying.* Except for a rise from 1985 to 1990, serious crime trends among nonwhite teenagers have been on the decline for 20 years—but major crimes among white adults have been surging steadily upward."[66] Youth homicide rates also decreased in California by 53 percent from 1990 to 1996. Yet in the 1980s, three-fourths of incarcerated youth were members of racial minority groups, and the confinement of minority youth increased by 80 percent in the 1990s.[67]

In addition, the fastest-growing rates of incarceration and detention are among women. Since 1980 the number of women entering prisons has doubled every seven to eight years.[68] In 2000 young women made up a quarter of juveniles arrested.[69] African American and Latina young women have the greatest spikes in incarceration rates.[70] Young women continue to suffer the consequences of the Progressive Era establishment of female delinquency as deviant sexuality. Although young women are less likely to be charged for sexual indiscretion today, they are overrepresented in status offenses, such as running away and incorrigibility, which are often based on suspected sexual offenses. The deinstitutionalization of status offenses in 1974 has reduced this unequal treatment of young women slightly, but, as Feld notes, many of the same status offenses charges have been reclassified as "simple assaults," relabeling anyone who commits them as delinquent.[71] Today, young women continue to be held for less serious offenses than their male counterparts.[72]

The criminalization of youth remains gendered, with young male members of racial minorities represented as perpetrators of crime and violence, and young female members represented as overtly sexual subjects. Young women of color—especially African Americans, Asian Americans, and La-tinas—have their own particular histories of sexual objectification and subjugation. Young African American women have overwhelmingly been represented as targets of intervention for social service programs to control their sexuality, especially in the form of teenage pregnancy prevention and treatment. Much like the working-class, immigrant young women of the Progressive Era, young African American women today are assumed to be sexually experienced and precocious, and the black teenage welfare mother was a favorite stereotype in the conservative backlash of the 1980s. Yet, until the 1970s, teenage pregnancy was not even mentioned as a social problem, and at that time birthrates were actually going down for this population.[73] Birthrates among teenagers aged fifteen to nineteen peaked in 1957 and declined between 1976 and the early 1990s.[74] Although teenage pregnancy is often posed as a problem of race—particularly for young African American women—Kristin Luker suggests that it is rather an issue of class, as an over-whelming number of young mothers live in poverty, and "poor women tend to be young mothers."[75] Yet the visibility of teenage pregnancy as a problem of young African American women also targets them as subjects of sexual intervention programs. Nathanson explains:

> Although recent changes in sexual behavior and pattern of family formation have been most marked among young women who are white, these young women are least likely to employ strategies of reproductive management that bring their behavior to public attention. The clients of strategies that select on the basis of *visible* sexual unorthodoxy—nonmarital pregnancy (in its later states) and nonmarital childbearing—are predominantly poor and of minority status. . . . This is, of course, a self-reinforcing process: the selection of poor and minority young women into formal programs for pregnancy adolescents further contributes to perceptions of the public and policy mak-ers that the problem of adolescent pregnancy *is* a problem of poor and minority adolescents.[76]

Similarly, young women of established social classes in the Progressive Era re-lied on less public forms of intervention to deal with premarital pregnancy in private, as opposed to working-class women, who were sent to reformatories.

Since the late nineteenth and early twentieth centuries, the intervention strategies, programs, and institutions to care for and control young people have taken new and not-so-new shapes and guises. Constant throughout, however, is the notion that young people are important subjects of care and control and a population in need of special intervention. The juvenile justice system today is the principal state institution aimed at regulating young people. But youth are also subject to a host of private and public programs (drug rehabilitation, military camps, teenage pregnancy prevention, sexual health) aimed at "fixing" them. Community-based youth activist organizations aimed at empowering youth view their programs diametrically opposed to such "kid-fixing" programs. But historical insight into the establishment of youth intervention strategies reveals how such diverse programs represent different sides (improve versus punish) of the same logic of social control. In other words, attempts to empower youth are intertwined with processes to criminalize them. Community-based programs today share an agenda with these past efforts in targeting poor and marginalized youth of color as a population in need of guidance away from improper behaviors and "bad" influences, and toward "fixing" them by ridding them of these problems. The poor, working-class European immigrants of the past have largely been replaced as targets of control by youth of color and immigrants from other countries. The idle young man has been transformed into a violent and hardened youth of color; the sexually precocious young female remains an object of moral concern, but she is now also a person of color. Thus the assumption remains that community-based intervention programs will keep young people from crime or sexual immorality.

In the contemporary moment, discourses and policies to control and manage youth are central to social policy. John Muncie and Gordon Hughes note: "In crucial respects, numerous aspects of social policy—whether regarding parenting, health, education, employment—appeared to have been captured within a youth justice discourse. Attempts to formulate 'joined up' partnership approaches have drawn on all manner of 'early interventions,' from pre-school education to parenting classes, into a crime control discourse. Crime prevention has in effect activated a simultaneous criminalization of social policy."[77] This criminalization of social policy hinges on managing the potential for disorder and misbehavior, or the management of youth to keep them from becoming "at-risk." In the next chapter, I focus on youth intervention strategies of empowerment found in community-based organizations and programs in the latter part of the twentieth century, strategies that are critical to the emergence of youth organizing and activism and their employment of affirmative strategies of social control.

Chapter 2

YOUTH ORGANIZING AND
THE NONPROFITIZATION OF ACTIVISM

A 1992 report funded by the Carnegie Corporation titled *A Matter of Time: Risk and Opportunity in the Nonschool Hours* sounded a fervent call to boost after-school and community-based programs in order to support youth and address urban decline. The document was extremely influential in reviving attention to the need for community programs and support for young people, especially among philanthropic foundations and nonprofit organizations. It mobilized the Evelyn and Walter Haas Jr. Fund to invest in and promote community programs for positive youth development and youth organizing. The foundation was also instrumental in financing the report that led to the passage of Oakland's Measure K in 1996, which set aside 2.5 percent of the city's unrestricted, general-purpose funds for after-school programs for children and youth.

The interest that the Carnegie report aroused in philanthropic circles in youth community programs significantly shaped the youth of color organizing movement that arose in the 1990s. Philanthropic investment also underscores two noteworthy points: (1) community programs were once again proposed as a positive strategy for redirecting young people's potential to engage in crime and delinquency; and (2) these programs were initiated by collaborations between state and private actors, like the collaborations that had supported youth programs in the late nineteenth and early twentieth centuries. However, youth intervention strategies of empowerment are significantly different in the 1990s: youth are understood to be active agents, responsible for their own empowerment and that of their communities. This is a notable distinction from traditional understandings of youth as passive receivers of intervention strategies. Programs aimed at improving young people to become better democratic subjects still rely on philanthropic and community organizations, but with the shift from a welfare state to a neoliberal state, the programs' roles as nonprofits shifted as well. The work of producing youth as actors responsible for themselves and their community now falls on the shoulders of a group of talented nonprofit employees.

My central concern in this chapter is to contextualize the embrace of youth organizing in the 1990s within these processes and to examine it as a mode of affirmative governmentality that stresses neoliberal principles of self-responsibility and community governance. Youth of color organizing arises as an innovative intervention strategy in youth social services and is heavily supported by a select group of private philanthropic foundations. It is less an organic, ad hoc, oppositional formation, but more appropriately situated within the field of youth intervention services. Although aimed at altering power relations and instigating institutional change, youth of color organizing nonprofits are nevertheless entangled in the state institutionalization of activism and neoliberal trends, which leads the nonprofits to follow business management models of efficiency and outcomes.

A Different Approach to "At-Risk" Youth

A Matter of Time was commissioned by the Task Force on Youth Development and Community Programs of the Carnegie Council on Adolescent Development. The report was designed to reflect the Carnegie Corporation foundation's emphasis on the role of promoting healthy adolescence (the period between the ages of ten and fifteen) for the nation. As part of a series of reports on youth, including their education and health, the 1992 document focused on strengthening the role of national and local youth organizations: "The purpose of this report, then, like the purpose of the task force itself, is to expand the scope and availability of developmentally appropriate, community-based services for young adolescents, particularly those living in high-risk environments, and to enhance public understanding and support of effective services for America's youth."[1] The report warned of dangers faced by young people in "high-risk communities": "Lacking a vision of a productive adulthood and constructive activities to engage them during nonschool hours, they [low-income adolescents] veer into another course of development. Some injure their health by using tobacco, alcohol, and other drugs. Some engage in premature, unprotected sexual activity, which the presence of AIDS now renders deadly. Some commit acts of crime or live in neighborhoods where fear of violence pervades their daily lives. Although all adolescents face at least some of these hazards, those who live in urban and rural poverty areas face a higher level of risks."[2]

Youth living in low-income, poverty-stricken areas were highlighted as "at-risk." This term was deployed in the 1970s and increasingly in the late 1980s and early 1990s, replacing other race- and class-based terms of the 1960s such as "culturally disadvantaged" or "culturally deprived."[3] The concept of young people and children "at-risk" had gained further currency with the release in 1983 of the report *A Nation at Risk*, sponsored by the US Department of Education, which instigated a panic over the poor quality of public education and unprepared schoolchildren. Although the term is not directly used in the report, the document underscored the need for federal intervention and monitoring of "at-risk" children and their parents, particularly poor and minority families, along with recommendations of higher standards and rigorous testing. "At-risk" is also applied to white, poor, and rural youth, but it has overwhelmingly come to represent poor, minority, and urban youth—who are deemed to be subjects "at-risk" and in need of intervention.

What is significant about the Carnegie report is that it promoted changing sensibilities about the subjectivity of "at-risk" youth. The report heralded a new approach of keeping these high-risk youth from peril by providing them with positive youth development opportunities via community programs. One of the observations made in the report was: "Current federal policy focuses primarily on intervening with young adolescents who are already in trouble, not on helping them keep out of it. Most federal dollars and technical assistance are aimed at crisis intervention, treatment of problems, and control of antisocial and criminal behavior, which leads to incarceration, often without meaningful rehabilitation."[4] The report was referring to traditional "kid-fixing" programs that borrow from the public health model aimed at crisis intervention and treatment. These programs conceptualize youth or adolescence as a distinct biological and psychological stage of human development filled with physical and emotional turmoil that goes hand in hand with risky behaviors. Take, for example, the charge of the Centers for Disease Control and Prevention's healthy adolescent division to "identify and monitor" six categories of risky behaviors, "including behaviors that contribute to unintentional injuries and violence; tobacco use; alcohol and other drug use; sexual behaviors that contribute to unintended pregnancy and sexually transmitted diseases (STDs), including human immunodeficiency virus (HIV) infections; unhealthy dietary behaviors; and physical inactivity."[5] In its section on "healthy people in every stage of life," the website of the Centers for Disease Control and Prevention does not include the above list of risky behaviors in any other age group other than that of adolescence. In this dominant model of "kid-fixing" youth services, young people are viewed as a special category of risk, in need of intervention programs to combat the vices of crime, violence, gangs, substance abuse, and sexual activity.

In contrast, the young people "at-risk" in the 1992 Carnegie report are presented as subjects in need of and in want of opportunities for positive development, thus underscoring a shift in youth subjectivities. Their potential for risk lies not in physical and sexual misbehaviors, but rather the negative influences of poverty, family, and/or neighborhood: "Although all adolescents face at least some of these hazards, those who live in urban and rural poverty areas face a higher level of risk. They are likely to have a lower level of personal and social support than their counterparts from more affluent families. . . . These outcomes can be reversed, if Americans decide to create communities that support families, educate adolescents for the global economy, promote their health, and provide opportunities for them during the nonschool hours."[6] Here we find discourses of youth *as risks* (that is, people at a vulnerable biological life stage or as perpetrators of crime) reframed as youth *at risk* (that is, people from bad neighborhoods and families). These "at-risk" youth of color are deemed to be valuable subjects who could become self-empowered with proper supports and opportunities. In this regard, they are unlike those populations designated as irredeemable and unworthy under neoliberal governance and positioned as, to use Katharyne Mitchell's words, resting "outside of risks."[7] But this does not mean that such youth are positioned far from such risks. Rather, poor, marginalized youth of color are conceptualized as a special category in which their risks loom larger than others; therefore, they are subjects in need of controlled activities to keep them from such dangers. The language of managing risk, either risky youth or those at risk, reveals youth intervention approaches as embedded in co-constitutive powers to enable and control.

In the 1990s, as in the Progressive Era, private philanthropists, state policymakers, academics, and practitioners saw community-based programs as the way to protect young people from their own potential for risky and delinquent behavior. This intervention strategy was also prevalent in the 1960s. For instance, the Ford Foundation's Gray Areas Programs focused on the development of youth programs to promote education, employment, and community participation as solutions for the "urban crises" and poverty in six locations.[8] Oakland was chosen for the first Gray Areas Program, which lasted from 1962 to 1966. The Ford Foundation sponsored the pilot in partnership with the city of Oakland to manage poor, "culturally disadvantaged" or "disadvantaged children" by explicitly focusing on improving their chances to avoid risks via educational and community programs.[9] It provided $2 million to subsidize public programs that focused on improving the chances of the city's young residents to participate fully in middle-class life by providing opportunities to remedy their "deficiencies."[10] These programs targeted largely African American youngsters and took the form of language development classes in Oakland public elementary schools, expanded recreation programs, youth employment training programs, and various other community participation programs.[11]

At the time the Ford Foundation was influenced by the work of Professors Richard Cloward and Lloyd Ohlin, who advanced a theory of opportunity for "lower-class youngsters" living in "lower-class neighborhoods."[12] Ohlin was recruited by Attorney General Robert Kennedy as an advisor, and Ohlin and Cloward's work had a significant impact on federal policies and programs such as the Juvenile Delinquency and Prevention and Control Act of 1961, which provided employment and work training for disadvantaged youth and directed resources to community organizations.[13] Other programs of the time that were informed by this premise of providing opportunities included Mobilization for Youth, Head Start, and the Job Corps.[14] Moreover, the work that the two professors did through Mobilization for Youth served as a major resource for President Lyndon Johnson's task force that wrote the Economic Opportunity Act, passed in 1964.[15] These collaborations between state policymakers, private foundations, and academics largely influenced youth programs and policies in the 1960s. This cooperation also established an intervention strategy for disadvantaged youth through a discourse of providing opportunities for improvement that would be repeated in future community-based programs.

The Carnegie report follows this past formula of youth management. The report outlined how "community-based youth programs can provide enriching and rewarding experiences for young adolescents."[16] It listed on one side, things "young adolescents needed," which were "opportunities to socialize with peers and adults," "opportunities to contribute to the community," and "opportunities to belong to a valued group." On the other side were things "community organizations offered," which were "group programs; mentoring and coaching," "safe places; constructive alternatives to gang involvement," "programs that incorporate the teaching of such critical life skills as goal setting, decision making, communicating, problem solving."[17] Following the tradition of the Progressive Era, the risks posed to economically marginalized and racialized youth are represented as an opportunity for improvement: "Risks will be transformed into opportunity for young adolescents by turning their nonschool hours into the time of their lives."[18]

But in contrast to attitudes in previous decades, the report openly embraced youth as subjects, not merely as objects of intervention, and advanced a concept of positive youth development that greatly influenced the growth of youth activist programs. The positive youth development framework gained ground in the late 1980s through investigative research of youth community programs by practitioners, researchers, policymakers, and foundations that resulted in a series of influential reports that were critical in shaping a new frontier of intervention for poor, "at-risk" youth.[19] One of the earliest of these reports, Karen Pittman and Marlene Wright's 1991 *Bridging the Gap: A Rationale for Enhancing the Role of Community Organizations in Promoting Youth Development*, was also commissioned by the Carnegie Task Force on Youth Development and Community Programs.[20] The Ford Foundation and Lilly Endowment funded the research for this report.[21] Pittman was also a member of this task force, and she has written numerous reports with Merita Irby and colleagues advancing a theory of positive youth development that was supported by various foundational initiatives and foundations including the Surdna Foundation and Evelyn and Walter Haas Jr. Fund.[22] The Ford Foundation's Community Youth Development Initiative also supported many of these reports. The goal of this initiative was "to enhance the ability of young people from economically disadvantaged communities to successfully transition from adolescence into responsible adulthood, economic self-sufficiency and engaged citizenship by building the capacity of low-income communities to create supportive environments."[23]

Although these reports do not use a single standard definition of positive youth development, its framework situates young people as central to the youth development process, in which their needs and skills are supported through community organizations. Pittman and Wright said: "We suggest that, first and foremost, the term *youth development* be attached firmly to young people, not solely to the institutions that serve them. Youth development should be seen as an ongoing, inevitable process in which all youth are engaged and all youth invested."[24] Some factors that help youth develop include providing basic and age-appropriate services and support; access to caring adults and safe spaces; building individual competencies; and emphasizing positive self-identity.[25] Moreover, proponents of positive youth development expanded this framework to include elements of youth engagement and youth action, emphasizing young people's active role and participation in community affairs.[26] Drawing on the convergence of youth development, civic engagement, and community development, youth action is loosely described as "young people making a difference in their communities—often in partnership with adults—to effect changes in things that are important to them and the community at large."[27] Pittman and her colleagues add, "Research on development increasingly emphasizes the importance of participation—choice and voice—for adolescents."[28]

Importantly, this positive youth development approach underscores youth agency, unlike in previous decades, when agendas providing young people with external supports and opportunities offered little mention of their active engagement. Here we find the explicit view of young people as capable subjects of their own empowerment, with an emphasis on supporting and providing opportunities for youth action. This shift is neatly summarized in a report published in 2003 by youth practitioners in support of positive youth development and youth organizing:

> The field of positive youth development yielded several important contributions. First, it pushed the field to develop new strategies and techniques for addressing young people's needs for civic engagement. Second, in seeking to do more than treat young people's individual "problems," youth development created a host of *collective empowerment techniques* that led to youth leadership development, youth civic engagement, and youth organizing. Third, and perhaps most important, once practitioners and thinkers broke away from the youth-as-problems-to-be-solved mold, a proliferation of new strategies and overlapping approaches emerged in the field of youth development [emphasis added].[29]

Some youth activist organizations, with their deliberate focus on collective action challenging social and power inequalities, may see their programs as distinct from the youth development organizations outlined above. However, the youth of color organizing movement and the nonprofit organizations and foundations supporting it arise from this paradigmatic shift in youth services, from a "kid-fixing" model to one of "positive youth development."

This turn to positive youth development in the field of youth services paved the way for youth organizing nonprofits to become attractive community programs for a select group of foundations that wanted to support youth activism. Sylvia Yee, the vice president of programs of the Evelyn and Walter Haas Jr. Fund in San Francisco wrote in a special journal issue titled "Community Organizing and Youth Advocacy": "The Carnegie report marked an exciting moment of paradigm shift. Philanthropy began to move away from an emphasis on 'fixing' troubled youth and toward supporting the healthy development of all young people. Across the country, local foundations absorbed the lessons of the Carnegie Report and began to act on them."[30] Recommendations in the report led the fund to give $16.5 million between 2003 and 2008 to support general youth development programs and to invest $4 million on youth advocacy programs.[31] There were other investors, too. For example, the Edward W. Hazen Foundation, committed to supporting youth leadership and development, made its first grant for youth activism projects in 1991 and between 1998 and 2003 allocated $2.5 million to these types of projects.[32] Youth of color activism and the nonprofits that support it directly benefited from this newfound philanthropic interest and are tied to this tradition of providing opportunities to manage and enable disadvantaged "at-risk" youth of color.

Despite these attachments to nonprofits and private foundations, youth of color organizing is often touted as an independent oppositional social movement. Its young participants are presented as vanguards of social justice movements: "Youth are articulating a new vision of feminism within low-income communities of color, redefining queer politics, forging intentional multiracial partnerships, and taking demands for immigrant rights beyond the workplace and into the community. In many of the anti-militarist demonstrations since September 11, youth groups assumed a high profile; no one scanning the legions of protestors would presume a deep apathy existed among young people today. Youth groups typically occupy the most progressive positions on education, criminal justice, environmental justice and the many other issues they confront."[33] Their activism often prompts parallels to the efforts of the 1960s: "Similar to the Student Nonviolent Coordinating Committee's (SNCC) contribution to the Civil Rights movement, young people today are vital to social change on these issues."[34] I am not calling into question the fact that youth of color organizing—with its ties to previous social movements to remedy social inequalities facing working-class families, immigrants, and communities of color—is taking steps to produce a more equitable society. Youth of color activism arose in in the 1990s in opposition both to state policies to restrict and reduce public services in education, employment, and health care; and to measures to criminalize and target young people. Yet such an idealized representation of youth organizing fails to situate young people's involvement as also being deeply entrenched in nonprofit structures and processes to institutionalize activism. The majority of community organizations supporting youth organizing were formed in the 1990s, and three-quarters of the groups have nonprofit status.[35] These groups remain heavily dependent on philanthropic foundations for support. I now turn to a closer look at the establishment of youth organizing nonprofits and the deployment of civil society as a mode of neoliberal governance, and the serious limits that these factors impose on activists' aims.

Youth of Color Organizing and Affirmative Governmentality

In 2000 the Funders' Collaborative for Youth Organizing (FCYO), a collaboration of national, regional, and local grant makers that promote the field of youth organizing, was formed. Lisa Sullivan, a youth activist and practitioner in the field, describes how the decision to establish FCYO was made by a few "activist-oriented program officers and foundation executives who had experience in youth and community development," hailing from foundations known to support social grassroots endeavors—namely, the Jewish Fund for Justice, Hazen Foundation, Ford Foundation, and Surdna Foundation.[36] These foundations were stimulated in part by the renewed national focus on community-based programs in the 1990s, as promoted by the Carnegie report, and in part by their own disillusionment with national community service programs that were politically neutral, such as AmeriCorps. In 1997 the Open Society Institute hosted a forum to introduce youth organizing to the larger funding community and attracted over seventy-five national, regional, and local grant-making institutions. Subsequent meetings were held over the next few years among foundation allies and key youth organizing practitioners, with a critical meeting in December 1998 leading to the formation of FCYO in 2000.[37] By 2007 FCYO had partnered with over forty-five philanthropic and practitioner organizations. According to its website, "the mission of the FCYO is to substantially increase the philanthropic investment in and strengthen the organizational capacities of youth organizing groups across the country."[38] Youth organizing was a deliberate investment made by a select group of philanthropic foundations to promote alternative youth intervention programs that incorporated political activism.

It is important to emphasize that the amount of funding earmarked for youth organizing programs constitutes small change in the field of youth services. Even within the realm of private foundations, only a few have wholeheartedly embraced youth organizing as a fundable project. A 2003 FCYO report states: "The majority of local and regional foundation resources, however, are dedicated to supporting traditional approaches to youth work—job training, community centers, after-school initiatives, and summer programs. Youth organizing continues to operate on the philanthropic margins, and youth organizing groups struggle to translate their work to a broader audience of skeptical funders."[39] In a 2002 essay, Sullivan wrote that FCYO's goal of raising $5 million was "a drop in the bucket compared to the resources that are likely to be invested in national service, youth development, mentoring, and social service delivery systems for youth over the next five years."[40] From 2003 to 2004, according to FCYO, the amount of philanthropic and public funds directed nationally at youth organizing programs made up less than 1 percent of the resources given to other youth development programs.[41]

The foundations that compose FCYO found youth organizing to be a worthy investment in turning potentially "at-risk" poor youth of color to become active political subjects because of their close proximity to risks. Almost 90 percent of the young people tied to youth organizing nonprofits are racial minorities, and 80 percent are from low-income families.[42] A 2003 FCYO report elaborates: "For young people growing up in low-income communities the challenges are often exacerbated by a number of factors: a lack of economic opportunity for their parents, family instability, inadequate schools, the prevalence of drugs, violence, and social isolation, and, in the case of ethnic and racial minorities, racism."[43] Despite the hindrances of racial marginalization and low socioeconomic status, youth organizing, with its attention to social justice, was touted as a more effective strategy of personal and community transformation for these young people because of their oppressed status. The report continues: "For marginalized youth, who are most isolated and frequently discriminated against, youth organizing has particular utility. Within youth organizing, marginalized youth find companionship, structure, and a critical framework for studying and understanding the world around them—connecting their public and private life. By helping young people see how their individual experiences, both positive and negative, are shared by others, young people participate in *group* efforts that lead to building *collective* power."[44] Yee confirms that youth organizing and advocacy "is a pathway to engagement that transforms the lives of young people, especially those who are alienated or marginalized."[45] We find here that youth organizing reiterates past management strategies to simultaneously enable and safeguard poor minority youth against risks. But it also draws on new affirmative strategies of self-empowerment and community responsibility.

For these philanthropic foundations and youth advocates in the early 2000s, investing in organizations that promoted youth organizing was viewed as a different—and better—strategy because its approach merged both positive youth development and community change. Take, for example, the 2003 report mentioned above. It is the first of FCYO's Occasional Papers Series on Youth Organizing. Titled *An Emerging Model for Working with Youth: Community Organizing + Youth Development = Youth Organizing*, it articulates the significance of youth organizing as a "collective empowerment strategy" because it combines both individual development and community social change outcomes.[46] Youth organizing promotes individual youth development outcomes of self-empowerment—such as building self-confidence, self-esteem, and a positive sense of identity—through meaningful adult and peer relationships in safe, comfortable spaces. These individual youth development skills could potentially be applied toward an analysis of social problems and community activism to offer double benefits—both to the individual and to the community. The report adds: "Youth organizing is meeting the complex needs of today's disengaged youth as young people from all walks of life develop new skills and apply them as they work to transform their communities."[47] Yee stated that what compelled the Haas Jr. Fund to encourage youth organizing is the fact that "in the pursuit of policy or social change outcomes, youth organizing and activism programs have not abandoned the broader youth development paradigm with its focus on individual development."[48] She adds: "The history of the Haas, Jr. Fund's involvement with both organizing and the youth development movement has led it to support programs with this dual bottom line: developing young people's individual capacities and advancing social change through collective action."[49]

Yet, under neoliberalism, individuals are not necessarily guaranteed the right to economic and social equality in the form of social programs and policies, regardless of the severity of their structural constraints (such as racism or economic inequality). Rather, they are given the opportunity to participate in the economic market, and thus attempt to improve their chances in life. Michel Foucault explains: "Social policy cannot have equality as its objectives."[50] He adds: "In short, [social policy] does not involve providing individuals with a social cover for risks, but according everyone a sort of economic space within which they can take on and confront risks."[51] All individuals in society, as in the free market, are supposedly afforded the opportunities to develop their human capital either "directly and as an individual, or through the collective means of mutual benefit organizations."[52] Those who lack adequate human capital can participate in programs and institutions set up to help them amass it.

Nonprofit organizations rely on the active and voluntary participation of marginalized and racialized groups. Miranda Joseph argues that nonprofits operate under the unequivocal and misguided belief that they are sites and locations of community, on which liberal subjectivities of choice and volunteerism are constituted and undertaken as an authentically grassroots experience.[53] Hence, failure to voluntarily participate is not only to bear, in the words of Nikolas Rose, "the risks posed to the individual themselves if they cannot adequately manage their life within the community, [but also] the risks the individual may pose to the community on account of their failure to govern themselves."[54] In the current moment of neoliberalism, the will to empower and be empowered is exercised as a mode of power intended to regulate and enable young people by encouraging them to participate in nonprofit programs meant to protect them from the risks of their environments and also from the threat of becoming "at-risk." Following this logic of self-governance and community responsibility, it becomes apparent that a citizen-subject's failure to act or help him- or herself justifies state intervention. It also legitimizes such individuals' criminalization (as gang members) and punishment (for example, being tried as an adult). Thus youth governance teeters uneasily between understandings of youth as a category in need of care and as a category in need of control.

Moreover, the turn to the community at the end of the twentieth century to solve social problems and the reliance on empowerment programs to build human capital skills of youth development both work to mask the central role of state power and the diffusive modes of neoliberal governance. In its employment of affirmative strategies of personal responsibility and community governance, this mode of governance also uses strategies of criminalization and punishment. Solutions to community problems, such as the violence and drug abuse that plague poor urban communities, are reached through voluntary antiviolence community task forces, adoption of drug-free zones, and partnerships in which local residents collaborate with law enforcement officers. The Violent Crime Control and Law Enforcement Act of 1994, passed in the Clinton administration, is a perfect example of simultaneous penal expansion and community crime prevention. By focusing on three policy sectors—police, punishment, and prevention—the act expanded the boundaries of criminalization by increasing the federalization of crime and justice, allocated $9.9 billion for new prison construction, and introduced an innovative approach to crime prevention: community policing. In an unprecedented move, the act stressed a new form of crime control and prevention, resulting in the creation of the Office of Community-Oriented Policing Services, which expanded community policing across the country with placement of more than 100,000 community police officers. The act also expanded the office's program that implemented experimental programs in local communities, including public education and media relations campaigns, Neighborhood Watch programs, town meetings, and community newsletters and websites.[55] The provisions of the act show how criminal justice has taken on the discourse of community responsibility, garnering the active participation of citizens in the enforcement of justice and prevention of crime. Control of neighborhood crime is relegated to collaborative community forms of governance and policing, reflecting the shift of state responsibility to the individual and community. In this mode of community governance, youth development skills are aligned with a neoliberal strategy to empower an ideal democratic subject—self-active, self-aware, and personally responsi-ble—while simultaneously targeting those subjects and making them re-sponsible for their own life risks and chances and their community's suc-cess or failure.

Youth of color organizing is integrally tied to this strategy of governance and technology of citizenship, and young people's efforts for social change are entangled in this web of relationships. Nonprofit youth organizations, charged with developing and improving the life chances of "at-risk" youth of color, are imbricated to neoliberal policies and reconfigurations of civil society that aim to manage and regulate the production of moral economic actors who are receptive to opportunities for self-empowerment and com-munity governance. Furthermore, this emphasis on the role of nonprofits to train marginalized youth of color to become self-empowered commu-nity leaders who will tackle the social and structural problems of racism and poverty places an undue burden on these nonprofits and the people they employ. Tributes to the power of youth of color organizing as a pro-gressive social justice movement have yet to contend with these relation-ships of power. For instance, Yee argues that the philanthropy "came to appreciate that a core of politically engaged and savvy activists capable of problem solving, altering power dynamics, and securing significant policy changes is the most important community asset for addressing discrimina-tion, racism, and poverty."[56] Yet it may be that youth organizing's real power is that it is a collective empowerment technique that can invest young people of color with the responsibility for taking action against the social problems facing their communities. Youth of color organizing echoes management strategies of the Progressive Era and the 1960s to promote community programs as a way of preventing youth delinquency and sexual immorality; it also reflects former collaborations between state and private actors to guide this process. But youth of color organizing differs in the emphasis placed on youth agency and in the transformation of civil society, particularly the significant rise of nonprofit organizations to enable and manage this activism, in the latter half of the twentieth century. I turn to these processes in what follows.

The Institutionalization of Activism

As I outlined in the introduction, although civil society is often positioned as operating outside of state regulation and political economy, and in opposition to state politics, civil society and specifically the nonprofit organizations that constitute it are not separate from these entities. What we know today as nonprofits have existed since the mid-seventeenth century, originating as colonial religious organizations. Nonprofit organizations in the United States grew exponentially during the late twentieth century.[57] Their numbers rose from 12,500 in 1940 to just under one million in 1989.[58] Currently there are over two million US nonprofits.[59]

The rise of nonprofit organizations in the latter half of the twentieth century is due in part to the civil rights movement and the government practice of contracting social services to nonprofit organizations. The activism of this period expanded state resources through Great Society social programs for medical care, welfare, education, housing, poverty, civil rights, and immigrants.[60] The subsequent ethnic power movements made claims on the state for racial representation and economic resources, explicitly forcing the state to concede to racial minority groups' demands.[61] The federal government addressed racial, social, and economic inequalities through grants and social policies. It also contracted with nonprofits to deliver social and public services. Yen Le Espiritu notes: "Between 1960 and 1968, the number of federal grant programs nearly tripled, from 132 to 379, and federal aid dollars more than tripled, from $7 billion in 1960 to $24 billion. . . . More important, the social policies of the Johnson years legitimized the claims of the disadvantaged by placing them on the national agenda."[62] Concessions to minority demands resulted in government funds directed at previously neglected ethnic minority groups and communities. For instance, in her historical study of Oakland's Chinatown and its institutions, Eve Ma observes: "In the late 1960s and early 1970s, the city and other governmental bodies for the first time took an active interest in Chinatown's well being, and began channeling money and programs towards the Chinese community."[63] She continues: "In addition to city attention, by 1980, Oakland's Chinatown was getting money from county, regional and federal sources. The federal government agencies had little interest in helping the Chinese community prior to the Kennedy era."[64]

Although these funds expanded the resources available to racial minority communities, community groups once rooted in radical aims of institutional change have either been met with state repression or co-opted into professionalized state institutions.[65] A familiar tale in the post–civil rights era is how these groups have been transformed into politically neutral nonprofits oriented toward the direct provision of services.[66] Driven by the need to secure funding from state, corporate, and philanthropic sources in the face of budget cuts, many ad-hoc oppositional groups professionalized themselves, becoming 501(c)(3) nonprofit organizations, a status often required for funding. As organizations competed for public and private funds, they were restructured to become legitimate and reputable institutions, transforming internal community and organizational dynamics and tempering once overt political aims. In the Asian American community, for instance, grants were used to reward well-established community organizations and agencies whose leaders exhibited skills in getting grants and had advanced degrees. This led to the rise of professional service workers, overwhelmingly middle-class second- and third-generation Chinese Americans and Japanese Americans, who in turn became leaders of these nonprofit organizations.[67] The professionalization, bureaucratization, and depoliticization of formerly radical and political groups into 501(c)(3) nonprofit organizations have legally limited their political activity, underscoring the nature of the "nonprofit industrial complex."[68] In the process of expansion and political legitimization, activists' demands for economic redistribution and political representation have been reduced to professional forms of advocacy, litigation, and lobbying. I do not mean to assert here that nonprofits cannot engage in political critiques of the state, and some of them make the most of their legally limited political activity. Rather, my critique echoes Wendy Brown's claim that redress made to marginalized groups often fails to recognize that the state is the perpetrator of their social injury.[69] In addressing social injury through mainstream political representation, incorporation, and redistribution, the state as a site of domination and oppression—and as a site in which to wage struggle and confrontation— disappears.

The coupled expansion and institutionalization of nonprofit organizations is also closely tied to the dismantling of the welfare state and rise of government contracting of social services to nonprofit organizations since the 1970s. The retrenchment of government spending on social services had a broad impact, adversely affecting education, housing, youth services, and many other areas.[70] Francis Piven and Richard Cloward note the erosion of the modest economic gains in the mid-1970s: "The Great Society programs that had provided resources and justification for black protest were stifled, their activities curbed, and their funds curtailed or eliminated in favor of new revenue-sharing or block grant programs."[71] Most of the social service programs were dismantled by the 1980s, especially under the Reagan administration, which reversed War on Poverty programs to wage a "war against the poor."[72] Thus, resources for youth community programs established during the 1960s were rich in promise but also short-lived. Robert Halpern explains: "Although President Johnson's indirect War on Poverty dramatically increased federal funding for services to children, most of that funding went either to early childhood services, especially Head Start; compensatory education programs; or initiatives for older youth."[73] Additionally, "most new federal funding also came with strings attached—a particular objective, strategy, or population or a requirement to collaborate with other institutions."[74]

This retrenchment of social services by the state has accompanied a government trend to increase contracts to nonprofit organizations to deliver social services. Prior to the 1970s the field of social services was characterized by independent private charities and a handful of government agencies. But, as Steven Smith and Michael Lipsky wrote in 1993, "today, social service provisions takes place through the unwinding of complex relations between legislative appropriations, government contracting, and implementation of public polices by means of nonprofit organizations dependent on public funds."[75] Government support comprises half, if not most, of the revenues of nonprofit service organizations, underscoring what Smith and Lipsky referred to as the "contracting regime." For instance, a 1982 national study undertaken by the Urban Institute found that the total federal, state, and local government spending on nonprofit programs in the San Francisco Bay Area equalled $1.1 billion.[76] At the same time the government outsourced publicly funded services, including youth programs, to local, community-based nonprofit organizations. Almost 40 percent of government spending for six key public services, including youth programs, was earmarked for nonprofit organizations. The result was that government agencies and nonprofits were given roughly the same share of funding to implement social services that in the previous decade had been handled solely by public agencies.[77] Moreover, as Smith and Lipsky observe, this "purchase-of-service system" by the government transfers state accountability to the private sector while pressuring its nonprofit contractors to conform to hegemonic state powers through policy provisions and funding requirements.[78]

This mutual dependence of state and private sectors challenges the common assumption that civil society is separate from the political state and market forces. Rather, nonprofits are a significant contributor to the political economy. In 1993 nonprofit organizations accounted for approximately 7.9 percent of the gross domestic product, and the operating expenditures of nonprofits increased almost fivefold between 1977 and 1998.[79] As of 1998, the nonprofit sector employed about eleven million people, making up over 7 percent of the US workforce.[80] Lester Salamon adds: "This means that paid employment alone in nonprofit organizations is three times that in agriculture, twice that in wholesale trade, and nearly 50 percent greater than that in both construction and finance, insurance, and real estate. . . . With volunteer labor included, employment in the nonprofit sector, at 16.6 million, approaches that in all branches of manufacturing combined (20.5 million)."[81] Nonprofits hence are squarely embedded in relations of capital. Joseph notes: "Nonprofits are supposed to be *not* for profit—the capital they accumulate cannot be distributed for profit—but they are also not non-capitalists and especially not anticapitalist."[82]

Added to these processes is the rise of private foundations. Philanthropic foundations have a long history of shaping social services and state policies in the United States, but their efforts have also expanded significantly in the latter part of the twentieth century. In 1955 private donations totaled $7.7 billion. This jumped to $39 billion in 1978 and $175 billion in 1998.[83] In the early 1960s, the number of foundations grew at a rate of 1,200 per year and they were promoted as tax shelters.[84] The Tax Reform Act of 1969 attempted to regulate foundations by requiring them to spend at least 6 percent of their net investment income and restricted their business operations to maintain their charitable purpose.[85] Donations to nonprofit organizations are tax deductible, however. The channeling of private, tax-sheltered funds to nonprofit organizations as charitable gestures serves to mask the economic inequality of capitalism, serves corporations through minimal redistribution of their wealth, and obfuscates the use of philanthropy as an instrument of social control to maintain the interests of capital and "hegemonize anti-capitalist populations."[86] For these reasons, scholars have pointed out, philanthropic foundations play a role in quelling social movements and reinforcing capital interests.[87] The Ford Foundation, for example, was notable for its interventions in social movements of the 1960s.[88] Robert Allen describes how the foundation's co-optation of the Congress of Racial Equality during the civil rights struggle tempered the group's revolutionary aims, assimilating them into reformist objectives of capitalism: "Black power was slowly but relentlessly coming to be equated with the power of black business."[89] However, in a study of philanthropic foundations, Jay Shiao argues against focusing on the role that foundations may have had in co-opting or instigating social movements. Rather, he claims that these foundations must be understood as operating within an institutional field with specific goals. In reference to the Ford Foundation, he writes: "I suggest that the many effects that foundations, especially Ford, have had on social movements are less compatible with narrow intentions to do harm or good than with the broader motivation to secure a particular type of relationship: *elaborating issues and piloting programs for eventual government adoption.* Demobilization, professionalization, local entrepreneurship, and nonprofit formation—all might be viewed as byproducts of initiatives to develop movements into potential public agencies or expand constituencies for existing public programs."[90] Shiao illuminates how philanthropic institutions such as the Ford Foundation sought to build collaborative relationships between state, private, and civil groups.

Just as state and private forces transformed civil society by domesticating political aims and redirecting collective action to the provision of politically neutral nonprofit social services, race and racial identities have been assimilated from their political roots into a state category of administration and intervention. To monitor funds directed at minority groups, in 1977 the Office of Management and Budget's Statistical Directive 15 "required all federal agencies to use five standard categories in program administrative reporting and statistical activities: American Indian or Alaskan Native, Asian or Pacific Islander, Black, White, and Hispanic."[91] Yen Le Espiritu and Michael Omi observe that the directive "has also shaped the very discourse of race in the United States, becoming the de facto standard for state and local agencies, the private and nonprofit sectors, and the research community. Directive 15 has also influenced group identity and community formation patterns."[92] In this process, once-political identifications such as "Asian American" have become state-validated identifications through which racial minority groups' political, economic, and social claims are staked and regulated.[93] This affirmation of racial identity and expansion of resources must also be understood as an effect of state power. Roderick Ferguson notes: "The historic arc that begins in the late 1960s signifies a profound change within modern institutions in the West. Administrative power had to restrict the collective, oppositional, and redistributive aims of difference at the same time that administrative power had to affirm difference to demonstrate administrative protocols and progress. We must read this affirmation as not simply a moment of encouragement but as a moment of subjugation."[94]

Similarly, the field of philanthropy reflected government processes to transform and institutionalize race from a political analytic attesting to social and economic inequality into a neutral category of individual empowerment and leadership. For instance, the Ford Foundation openly denounced the "Black nationalism" of the 1960s and instead promoted "Black professionalism."[95] Shiao describes the shift away from funding more-progressive black organizations: "During the 1980s, however, the Ford Foundation, along with the Carnegie Corporation and the Rockefeller Foundation, appear centrally in articles promoting minority self-reliance and new kinds of leadership among people of color."[96] Philanthropic foundations, like the state, are central to the relations of power and process to mitigate activism and depoliticize racial identities. In sum, civil society—particularly nonprofit organizations—does not exist outside of the hegemonic powers of the political state or its relations of capital to institutionalize political activism.

The Nonprofitization of Youth of Color Organizing

Youth organizing nonprofits are securely tethered to the relations of power that are embedded in capital and that deploy nonprofits as a governmental technology. Seventy-five percent of community programs that support youth organizing maintain nonprofit status, and 98 percent of youth organizing nonprofits are dependent on private foundations.[97] Youth organizing nonprofits differ from traditional youth service providers in that they rely heavily on private foundational sources, not public funds. But these organizations, like their state-funded counterparts, nevertheless operate within relations of power that institutionalize and nonprofitize activism. Although many of the foundations that support youth organizing nonprofits are described by some practitioners as progressive, youth activist organizations find themselves in tension with these funders' subdued approach to youth social change practices that are too closely bound to the promotion of individual youth development. Additionally, these philanthropic foundations reflect larger trends in political economy, adapting neoliberal free-market principles that continue to professionalize activist-oriented organizations.

This latter point is evidenced in foundations' promotion of efficient business management strategies and in the market-oriented outputs and outcomes from the nonprofits they fund. Sullivan warned of this:

> For better or for worse, the social movements of the 1960s and 1970s have been incorporated into the legislative and bureaucratic framework of the nonprofit sector, and this has important, albeit rarely discussed, ramifications for how this generation of social change agents leads and manages. Fighting for social justice in the 21st century as a well resourced nonprofit requires understanding first and foremost the legal and tax codes that determine how a not-for-profit *business* operates. This generation of youth activists and organizers must wrestle with the fact that the structures in which they operate are businesses that require basic management practices, strategic plans, and fund development strategies for sustainability.[98]

For many youth organizing practitioners, their vision of social change and activism can be dampened by the mundane tasks of reading through calls for proposals and balancing budgets. These organizations are dependent on private foundations whose funds are limited, tenuous, and often restricted to specific projects, leaving the organizations' day-to-day operations unstable. A FCYO report noted that during 2004 and 2006, "100% of the respondents experienced changes in funders' priorities or cycling out of funding," and that "75% experienced reduction in funding due to foundation cutbacks."[99] Even FCYO, dedicated to the long-term project of youth organizing, doles out only $60,000 to $250,000 annually, and in amounts ranging from $10,000 to $60,000 per youth organizing nonprofit, well under the organizations' total annual budgets.[100] The majority of youth organizing nonprofits have budgets under $350,000.[101] During the time I worked with AYPAL, the group's annual budget was larger, and because of its organizational structure, its funding sources were more diverse than those of nonprofits that relied heavily on foundations known to support youth organizing.[102] The contingency of funding for community programs reinforces critiques of philanthropic foundations, which tend to fund a larger number of nonprofit organizations for smaller amounts each, provide short-term grants, and shy away from providing core program support—all of which thwarts the political work in which activist organizations are engaged.[103] Evident in such practices are not only the financial constraints facing youth organizing nonprofits, but also their relationship to capital.

The resulting challenges faced by youth organizing groups are summarized in a 2007 FCYO-sponsored report:

[Youth organizing groups] are heavily dependent on foundation funding, while still in the start-up phases of developing multi-year fundraising plans, cultivating individual donors and exploring non-foundation resources, such as investments and income-generating enterprises. Despite their strong reliance on foundation funding, all groups experience challenges when it comes to finding an appropriate philanthropic fit or niche. Community organizing/ social justice funders view their work as a mere corollary to adult organizing. Meanwhile, progressive youth development funders view youth organizing as "too political." As such, groups often have to cobble together small, one-time grants from various foundations.[104]

Although there is much enthusiasm and promise in discussions of youth of color organizing as an innovative and progressive social justice movement among its practitioners and funders, more attention is needed to the fact that structurally, these organizations are heavily dependent on private foundational support to sustain their work. Recently, FCYO has attempted to address the challenges that funding limits posed to youth organizing groups through its 2010 Regenerations: Leadership Pipeline initiative by providing funds to expand organizational capacity and increasing its general operating support for selected youth organizing nonprofits.[105] However, during the time I conducted my research in the early 2000s, such shortcomings were not readily acknowledged. In the book's conclusion, I examine recent developments in FCYO, particularly the leadership pipeline initiative, to comment on the current state of youth organizing.

Moreover, the role of youth organizing nonprofits in producing social change by training young people in community organizing and leadership skills is constrained because such groups and their funders have different understandings of the impact and goal of youth organizing. The tension between philanthropic fit and youth organizing aims is most evident in what FCYO has recognized as "bridging the youth development–youth organizing divide."[106] This friction was discussed at a meeting I attended in San Francisco with a staff member of AYPAL in April 2003. The purposes of this meeting, the first of a two-part Dialogues for Youth-Led Community Change conference sponsored by FCYO, were to foster relationships among foundation officers and youth organizing practitioners and (according to the agenda distributed at the meeting) to facilitate "deeper and mutual discussion on critical issues facing the youth development/community change field." It became apparent early in the meeting that the primary issue at hand was the different perceptions among philanthropic foundation representatives and youth organizing practitioners regarding what constituted youth developmental outcomes. In both the small and large group discussions that ensued, youth organizing practitioners explained to foundation officers that it was difficult to parse out and summarize, in an annual report, what constituted individual youth development outcomes as opposed to social and political outcomes, because the practitioners saw them as intertwined. The individual skills such as leadership, self-confidence, and the ability to tell right from wrong were not separate from the political skills of organizing a direct action, dealing with the media at a press event, or developing an oppositional critique of capitalism. This point was not new, and I heard Jason, an AYPAL staff member, repeatedly say that youth organizing goes hand in hand with youth development and that youth organizing is a type of youth development.[107] Yet the practitioners at the meeting argued that the funders did not count youth organizing, with its sometimes abstract outcomes, as a legitimate youth development measure. A foundation officer sympathetic to the practitioners conceded that the board members of his foundation, like those members of other foundations represented at the meeting, often thought of youth development in terms of more tangible outcomes. For instance, board members hoped that young people's participation in youth organizing groups would result in educational attainment (such as better grades and a desire to pursue higher education) and financial stability (such as gaining job skills or entrepreneurial motivation).

I heard a discussion similar to the one at the FCYO meeting occur between a representative of a public funding agency and AYPAL staff during a midyear review. The agency's funding officer acknowledged the accomplishments of AYPAL as an organization and its ability to affect community change. Yet she brought attention to AYPAL's results in a survey required of all funding participants. Noting a survey item ("Because of the program their ability to do better in school improved") on which AYPAL scored a mere 29 percent, the officer said that all youth programs, including those featuring youth organizing, should be able to produce a quantifiable improvement in educational outcomes. These conversations reveal the pressure placed on youth organizing nonprofits to follow affirmative youth management strategies that shape young citizen-subjects into self-responsible and self-governing individuals who can improve their life chances and reduce their risks in a neoliberal order. But it also illuminates the resistance of this individualizing focus by practitioners who stressed collective action and the social implications of youth organizing.

For many youth organizing practitioners who interact with young people on a daily basis, it is not easy to meet the challenge of promoting both social change outcomes and individual youth development. Training youth to become community leaders and political activists is hard enough, but practitioners must also attend to young people who may be in need of direct services such as psychological counseling, educational tutoring, and substance abuse treatment. Some of the "star" youth in AYPAL, who were the most articulate speakers at rallies and meeting and who could explain the structures of power and inequalities to reporters at press conferences, were among the most poorly performing students at their schools, maintaining below-average grades. Very few staff members felt equipped to properly meet the developmental needs of young people. One told me: "Most of us come from left-leaning community youth organizing groups, and we don't have the knowledge and skills of youth development language and youth development outcomes, and we need training on this." AYPAL staff members, myself included, had varying opinions about how much attention should be paid to youth development skills as opposed to youth organizing, but regardless of our differences, we found ourselves doing both. A 2010 FCYO report of youth organizing confirmed this: "100% of groups that responded to our online survey are providing youth development supports as part of their youth organizing programs."[108] The report noted that organizations were attempting to better integrate youth development skills with youth organizing skills, especially in the areas of academic and emotional or mental support and of media relations, but that many of the organizations were left to provide young people with these supports informally. It is clear that youth organizing nonprofits had to manage and continue to manage, the expectation that they would do both tasks effectively and efficiently. Moreover, they are doubly accountable—first to the young people, and second to their funders.

In short, although youth organizing programs are positioned as part of a progressive social justice movement, they are intertwined with the institutionalization of youth services aimed at "fixing" and empowering "at-risk" youth of color to become better citizen-subjects. The organizations' activism is not only bound by the nonprofitization of activism, but it is also restricted by the generosity of the private foundations that fund them and that, in requiring accounts of progress from them, have traditionally reinforced capitalist aims and the social status quo.

Nonetheless, AYPAL, like many other youth organizing groups, worked within these nonprofit structures and the expectations placed on youth serving agencies. For instance, when the group received a grant specifically earmarked to conduct workshops on drug and violence prevention, I worked alongside AYPAL staff members to find a creative solution to tackle the narrowly defined approaches to "fixing" youth. In addition to delivering the required typical "don't do drugs" and "don't fight" messages that target individual young people as the problem, we expanded the curriculum to analyze drug abuse as a structural issue and to explore violence at the levels of the community and the state. We devised six workshops that were organized around how "drugs destroy communities and movements" and how violence is used to "divide and conquer." The drugs workshops engaged young people in a discussion of how drugs are traditionally spoken of as a personal problem (such as "it's his fault, he's a drug addict") and pointed out the devastating consequences of drugs on individuals and families. But we extended the discourse to include the social and community impact of substance abuse on movements for collective empowerment and social change by bringing up two historical examples, the Black Panthers in Oakland and the Opium Wars between China and England. Workshops also focused on the alcohol and tobacco corporations' accumulation of capital at the expense of individuals and the role of advertising in promoting substance abuse. In the workshops, we reminded young people that AYPAL was about community building and observed that to use drugs was to support a system designed to "break down communities." Similarly, the goal of the violence prevention workshops was to "identify forms of violence in our communities and how it works to divide us" by expanding violence from individual acts of aggression or anger to include gender violence, violence as a result of racism and classism, and different forms of state violence such as militarism and police brutality. These forms were then summarized and posted on a "wall of violence." During the last workshop, young people dismantled the wall and participated in skits that provided not only practical skills for avoiding violence but also pointed out the forms of state violence used to divide and conquer, and gave advice to young people on how to avoid getting caught up in the hands of "the man."

Through these workshops, AYPAL thus met funding requirements to engage young participants in drug and violence prevention that was not limited to traditional approaches to managing "at-risk" youth. And more important for its funders, AYPAL was able to provide evidence of outcomes in hard numbers that reported significant reduction in drug use and violent behavior, as measured in the pre- and post-surveys administered to 2youth. In AYPAL's 2001 yearly report to funding agencies, its young pparticipants reported a 40 percent decrease in their use of alcohol, tobacco, and other drugs; a 29 percent decrease in engagement with violent activities (including fights, carrying weapons, and involvement in gangs); and a 13 percent improvement in staying clear of "other risky behaviors" such as stealing, planning to run away, and being suspended from school. Thus, AYPAL worked within the institutional constraints of promoting individual youth behavioral outcomes while remaining rooted in the social justice aims of youth organizing.

The reality for the field of youth organizing and the goals and aims of the nonprofits and foundations that support them is that the two sides are often at odds with each other. Such differences among philanthropic officers and youth organizing practitioners were glaringly apparent at the earliest stages of youth organizing nonprofit formations. Sullivan describes the decisive meeting in December 1998 that served as the impetus to create

FCYO among interested foundation officers and youth organizing groups: "Funders seemed to have assumed that all youth agreed on the defining principles of youth organizing, but there was actually little agreement on core principles, strategies, goals, and values of their work. Funders also seemed anxious to have youth organizers define their work in a manner that would play well at trustee board meetings. Youth organizers were pointing to the lack of money to effectively do organizing work, while funders were asking about tools for program reporting and evaluation."[109] This evident strain emphasizes the pressure felt by youth organizing practitioners when faced with the demands of their funders, who themselves are driven by a desire for concrete outcomes from their investment. Although youth organizing is viewed as an alternative to and better than traditional youth development programs, funders remain tied to paradigms that measure improvement in individual human capital skills and that view community programs as an intervention strategy against youth delinquency and young people's exposure to risks. These challenges underscore the very real difficulties and obligations that nonprofit organizations and their staff face in implementing youth organizing as a lasting movement for social change. In short, the project of youth organizing illuminates larger social forces that have given civil society the responsibility for state-sponsored social services, creating a situation in which nonprofit organizations are called on to be more self-reliant, efficient, responsible, and effective institutions.

In expressing such a critique, my intent is not to devalue or disregard the real and important work that young people, the practitioners who work with them, policymakers, and funders are doing every day on the ground to challenge the myriad social inequalities facing young people. Nor is it to suggest that community programs that promote youth organizing or other youth development services are overly limited or unnecessary. I can attest to the fact that, in challenging the structures and relations of power in their workshops on sexism, racism, and colonialism, AYPAL staff created spaces in which young people could learn about systemic sources of inequality as well as critically articulate their experiences of oppression and inequalities.[110] These outcomes were not necessarily in opposition to traditional youth development outcomes, nor did they embrace particular techniques of empowerment. Ruth Nicole Brown eloquently argues for the necessity of spaces, such as Saving Our Lives Hear Our Truths (SOLHOT), that celebrate black girlhood among girls who are often marginalized by working against imperatives designed to control or improve their lives.[111]

My purpose in laying out the particular history and sociopolitical context in which youth organizing arose is to question the uncritical representation of youth of color activism as an unfailing solution to social change. It is to critically examine the collaborations between funders, policymakers, academics, and youth experts in their advocacy for investment in nonprofit youth organizations that aim to shape marginalized youth of color to become particular kinds of empowered citizen-subjects, and through that examination to reveal the tensions inherent in political organizing that is wedded to the state. It is to present an analysis that did not come readily during my time with AYPAL but developed afterward in my close attention to larger affirmative powers of youth governance and its relationship to the nonprofitization of activism. Youth of color organizing is not a panacea for social injustice and inequality; rather, it is the latest technique in a long line of youth management strategies. The next chapter examines the real impact of youth organizing in challenging power relations and producing concrete social change despite such limitations, through ethnographic details about AYPAL youth's participation in the campaign to halt the expansion of juvenile hall in Alameda County. Concomitantly, I also explore the relations of power that restrict the possibilities of this youth of color activism.

Chapter 3

ORGANIZING AGAINST YOUTH
CRIMINALIZATION

On March 9, 2001, the *Oakland Tribune* reported: "Red-faced probation department officials issued a press release this week saying figures they sent to the state were wrong, and correct numbers actually show assaults of minors on each other dropped 27 percent last year over the previous year."[1] Alameda County's probation department officials had erroneously reported an increase in youth violence of 64 percent in the department's request for $54.2 million from the California State Board of Corrections to rebuild and upsize the existing juvenile hall possibly in Dublin, a suburb southeast of Oakland. Outraged by the news, local youth activist organizations, led by members of Youth Force Coalition and the Books Not Bars Project of the Ella Baker Center for Human Rights, organized a press conference and protest on March 15 to call attention to the proposal to expand the facility. In attendance were young people from AYPAL along with their peers—mostly African American and Latino/a youth—who were participants in various youth activist nonprofit organizations in the Bay Area. The boisterous group of thirty-five or so activists gathered in front of the county's probation department near downtown Oakland to demand that the chief probation officer deny the county's proposal to build a "mega-juvi" big enough to hold 540 juveniles. Chanting "Books not bars!" and "Schools not jails!," the group tried to gain entry into the probation department to personally hand the chief a letter against the expansion proposal and protest the use of fraudulent statistics on youth violence as a basis for the proposal. Intimately familiar with the effects of increased state presence in the form of police surveillance in their schools and neighborhoods, zero-tolerance policies, and rising incarceration rates, these young people expressed their frustration with the blatant misuse and distortion of data by city officials. They pointed to the false data as further proof of the state's intention to criminalize youth of color. This action at the probation department marked the first of many in the campaign to stop the expansion of the juvenile hall, dubbed the "Super Jail."

The campaign officially named "Stop the Super Jail" took many dramatic twists and turns during the two years that the coalition needed to ultimately thwart the county's plan to build a larger juvenile hall. The success of the campaign against the Super Jail depended on the organizing efforts of hundreds of youth of color, many who were members of Youth Force Coalition, a Bay Area collaborative made up of more than twenty local youth organizing groups, including AYPAL. The young people tackled and successfully fought one of the most important issues facing youth of color at that time—the rapidly expanding prison-industrial complex. The coalition's ability to halt the expansion of juvenile hall in a period of record-breaking growth in the numbers of prisons and prisoners (over 2.3 million in 2008) in the United States is a testament to the power and potential of the youth of color organizing movement to mobilize in opposition to the state, despite the movement's attachments to nonprofit institutions.[2] In the previous chapters, I have discussed the relations of power in which youth organizing programs are posed as an empowerment strategy to redirect youth of color from potential criminal behavior and delinquency. I have outlined the limitations of youth of color organizing, its relationship to neoliberal modes of governance, and its embeddedness in state power. Yet in mobilizing against the Super Jail, activists directly confronted state processes to criminalize, target, and punish them because they were youth of color, rejected constructions of themselves as "super-predators," and expressed political resistance against such state efforts through a shared politicized and oppositional identity as "youth of color." In spotlighting state officials' use of false statistics to legitimize youth incarceration, young people questioned the usually unquestioned assumption of youth of color's criminality and delinquency. Their reasoning disputed the logic of neoliberal governance to privatize crime as the responsibility of a "bad" young person of color as opposed to making it the responsibility of the state to protect and invest in its young people. Their activism also revealed youth incarceration as a mode of state violence and punishment by exposing the central fallacy in state arguments for expanding youth incarceration: the unprecedented rise in youth violence and crime.

This chapter discusses youth of color activism against state efforts to expand a youth incarceration facility. The campaign shows that the young people's participation in youth activist programs was not merely a management strategy to keep them from delinquency and crime, but rather involved challenging state processes to criminalize and penalize them as targets of state control. I also examine how the campaign against the Super Jail revealed the compartmentalization of race and racial identities as a management strategy of neoliberal governance. Specifically, AYPAL youth's active participation in the campaign was critical in the victory as AYPAL was a prominent organizational partner within the Youth Force Coalition, and two AYPAL staff members were part of the tactical strategy team, the decision-making core of the campaign against the Super Jail. More important, AYPAL youth were a large and visible force (often making up more than half of the participants) at most actions against the Super Jail; pictures of AYPAL youth were frequently featured on the front pages of local newspapers during the campaign. Images of them at Super Jail protests were also featured in a DVD that documented the growing prison-industrial project and activism against it.[3] As one member aptly summarized the campaign actions, "Out of the seventy-five youth there, sixty of them are AYPAL!" They participated in numerous protest rallies, attended meetings of the Alameda County Board of Supervisors, traveled to meetings of the California Board of Corrections in San Diego and Sacramento, pressured elected officials who supported the expansion with phone calls and public demonstrations, and informed the public about the expansion in grassroots, door-to-door visits. Yet campaign discourses about youth incarceration and criminalization rarely mentioned Asian and Pacific Islander youth. In many descriptions of the campaign and at many campaign actions, these youth were overlooked as targets of state incarceration or criminalization unlike their African American or Latino/a counterparts. Rather, juvenile injustice was discussed and coded as a "black and brown" issue.

"Stop the Super Jail" campaign organizers drew on a familiar panethnic "people of color" identity often used in the post–civil rights era to challenge the state in order to ensure racial and political representation and redirect resources to youth empowerment (for example, "schools not jails"). Yet as I have discussed, this rights-based framework of demands for racial representation and redistribution of resources has been managed and reshaped by the state, as evidenced in the nonprofitization of racial minority groups' demands and the institutionalization of activism. The failure of other youth of color activists to recognize Asian and Pacific Islander youth as targets of state criminalization and violence reveals how race and identity politics are affirmed as depoliticized state categories. The response of

AYPAL youth illuminates how they grappled with this normalization so as to employ racial identities for political activism.

"Schools, Not Jails!"

Discussions about building a new juvenile hall in Alameda County began as early as 1992, when safety questions were raised about the facility's crumbling infrastructure and its location on a major earthquake fault line. The momentum to build and the movement to oppose the new center both took hold in earnest in 2001, when the county's probation department requested a total of $54.2 million in two separate proposals to build a larger juvenile hall outside of Oakland. Activists were not necessarily against a new facility; rather, they were against the county's expansion proposal and proposed location of the facility. The exact capacity and locale of the proposed structure changed often in the course of the campaign. The original proposal was to accommodate 299 beds; at one point, 540 beds were recommended instead. The original proposal was to locate the new facility in San Leandro, a city bordering Oakland to the south; then the proposed location was a sixty-acre parcel in Dublin, a suburb approximately thirty miles southeast of Oakland.[4] For the activists, the proposal to build the new center adjacent to Santa Rita Jail in Dublin, the third largest incarceration facility in California and the fifth largest in the nation, symbolized the pinnacle of the prison-industrial complex—the interlocking system of juvenile and adult institutions. In May 2003 the Alameda County Board of Supervisors finally voted to build a new facility near the original proposed location with a capacity of 330 to 360 beds. The new facility opened in April 2007 just down the hill from the old one, holding 300 beds initially but with the capacity to add another 60 beds.

The formal "Stop the Super Jail" campaign began when members of the Youth Force Coalition decided to tackle the issue after one of the group read about the misuse of crime figures to justify the expansion of the juvenile hall in Alameda County, as reported by Donna Horowitz in the *Oakland Tribune*.[5] The Books Not Bars Project of the Ella Baker Center for Human Rights—a national organization that challenges human rights abuses in the US criminal justice system, with a specific interest in the growing prison industry in California—joined the Youth Force Coalition in the campaign. Membership in the coalition waxed and waned during the campaign, but the Books Not Bars Project and the Youth Force Coalition were the official leaders throughout. The coalition is one of the many groups that make up the dense network of youth activist organizations in the Bay Area. Founded in 2000, it was one of the four youth groups of the Youth Empowerment Center, which was located in a warehouse in West Oakland. The coalition engaged various youth organizing nonprofits to work together on youth-related campaigns such as the protest against the Super Jail; the other three groups in the center, including the Underground Railroad and School of Unity & Liberation, equipped young people with political education and training in cultural arts for activism. Hip-hop was a popular cultural medium in the political protest against the Super Jail. Surrounded by a nexus of underground hip-hop collectives and a tradition of using hip-hop in progressive politics in the Bay Area, young people integrated spoken word and rap performances and used graffiti-style art in their protests.[6] Large public rallies called "Upset the Setup" and "Not Down with the Lockdown: Super Jam to Stop the Super Jail" featured hip-hop and break-dance performers, among them AYPAL youth.

Many of the young people involved in the campaign were connected to youth activist nonprofit organizations that emerged in the late 1990s and 2000s, as recounted in the previous chapter; however, the organizers also drew on the legacy of activism in Oakland. The local youth organizing movement culled tactics and strategies of protest from past social movements, such as the Black Panthers and Third World student movements.[7] Namely, the coalition's opposition to a larger and more distant facility used a strategy of demanding rights from the state reminiscent of this past, expressed in a demand for representational rights as "youth of color" and for the redistribution of resources from incarceration to youth empowerment (specifically, through an investment in schools and education).

For the activists against the Super Jail, the proposal to build a juvenile facility that could accommodate more than the existing facility's 299 beds at a time when youth crime was declining only confirmed the state's efforts to criminalize and target young people. A slogan often heard from activists in speeches and rallies during the campaign was, "If they build it, they will fill it!" The phrase underscored the state's presumption and projection of youth of color criminality and inevitable punishment. A seasoned African American activist at one of the campaign rallies declared that building a larger facility when youth crime rates were going down meant only one thing—young people were assumed to be guilty. She said: "The Super Jail is meant for young people here, anybody between ten [and] seventeen today or kids who haven't even been born. That is who this facility is for . . . it's for y'all. That's why we came out [against it], and that is why you are here. And we will continue to come out to stop it. Because you are against it. And for the older people here, it is because they are building that for our children, for our nieces and our nephews. And half of us already got people locked up in the system, half of us have our children [there]. . . . [We] have been abandoned by the Board of Supervisors and the State of California." Her words reinforce Ann Ferguson's claim that cultural representations of youth of color, in particular black children, are "adultified," with the innocence of their childhood replaced with representations of them as grown criminals.[8] In arguing that a larger facility was not only unnecessary but also unwarranted, activists challenged the common perception of young people as criminals or as being likely to commit crimes.

Moreover, the organizers against the Super Jail adamantly argued for a smaller number of beds on the premise that a bigger center was correlated with a statistically false rise in youth violence. As I explained in chapter 1, youth crime has decreased nationally since 1980. The drop in youth violence in Alameda County by 27 percent between 2000 and 2001 (as noted in the *Oakland Tribune*), specifically in assaults by juveniles on juveniles, mirrors this national trend.[9] The national decline in youth crime and violence, however, has had an inverse effect on youth incarceration and criminalization. In the 1990s and early 2000s, increased state resources were devoted to expanding juvenile incarceration facilities. This was aided in part by President Bill Clinton's approval in 1994 of using federal funds to build new juvenile facilities and expand existing ones across the United States. The national trend to upsize juvenile halls parallels the increase in adult correctional facilities, backed by policymakers under the slogan of getting "tough on crime." Between 1984 and 2007, California alone built twenty-three new prisons (compared to building only twelve new prisons between 1852 and 1964), which cost $280 million to $350 million apiece.[10] A report by the National Council on Crime and Delinquency in 2001 stated: "Now, the Legislature [in California] through the Board of Corrections has provided construction grants for new juvenile facilities in 40 of the 58 counties. California is increasing its capacity to detain youth by 50 percent, adding 3,150 new beds, in addition to replacing 1,300 existing detention beds. The growth in detention is fueled by old crime trends when the number of juvenile arrests was at their peak. In the past ten years, felony juvenile arrests in California declined by 45 percent."[11]

In addition to challenging the state's plan to incarcerate young people based on the unproved potential of youth crime, as demonstrated in the battle over bed capacity at the new juvenile hall, the activists highlighted the racial inequalities found in the process of youth criminalization and the effects of incarceration. A campaign flier noted: "People of color get harassed more by the cops, are often targets of racism in the courts and are consequently disproportionately incarcerated. In Alameda County, African-American children represent roughly 15% of the county's population but are almost two thirds of the youth detained in Juvenile Hall. More beds in the hall will mean even more kids of color on lock-down." The flier echoes the well-documented racial inequalities of the juvenile justice system that overwhelmingly contains members of racial minority groups, particularly African Americans. African American youth made up 40 percent of the population in juvenile halls in 1997, although they made up only 15 percent of the national youth population.[12] By calling attention to the racial disparities of youth incarceration, the activists underscored how "youth of color was criminalized and youth of color was racialized."[13]

Many of the young people in AYPAL, like others in the campaign against the Super Jail, spoke out about being targets of state criminalization and incarceration as racialized and criminalized youth of color. In particular, young Mien (Southeast Asian) men—a population whose incarceration rate was rapidly rising in Oakland—often told me about police officers "stopping them for no reason" while walking to and from school and questioning them about gang affiliations. Although most AYPAL members were not caught up in the juvenile system, they had friends and family members who were, and they were intimately familiar with the process of youth of color criminalization and incarceration. In addition, a young Samoan male who joined AYPAL after he was released from juvenile hall spoke at campaign rallies about his experiences of police surveillance. These occurrences reinforce the overt criminalization and targeting of the so-called super-predator youth of color—coded as male. Nevertheless, young people were also keenly aware of the number of females affected by incarceration. In fact, young women are the fastest growing population to be incarcerated and detained, and arrest patterns for young women are overwhelmingly centered on social control of their sexuality. Venus, a Filipina American in AYPAL, spoke at a large action against the Super Jail about the criminalization and targeting of youth of color like her: "As you can see, I am a young poor woman, and I am a target and I am just fucking tired of being set up. I'm tired of being put in the set up of being miseducated and not being given a job." Venus articulated here not only her feelings of being a target as a racialized youth of color but also her understanding of larger educational and economic inequalities. The county's plan to build a larger incarceration facility was understood as linked to other state and local policies—such as antigang task forces, and the presence of armed police officers on school campuses— to control so-called delinquent and deviant behaviors of youth of color.

An analysis that accounts for the interlocking policies and efforts target- ing racialized "at-risk" youth of color exposes a neoliberal approach to youth criminalization and punishment. Youth activists described youth crime not just as a consequence of wrongful individual choices but also as a structural process of youth criminalization. A common slogan on protest signs was: "Don't Blame the Youth, Blame the System," accompanied by chants such as "The county, the state, why they gotta hate?" Jennifer Tilton describes youth activism against the Super Jail as an effort to counter the dominant neoliberal agenda: "The image of dangerous youth often served to shrink a vision of public responsibility for social welfare, since it was easy to blame faulty families for 'disrespectful' young people running the streets."[14] As Nikolas Rose notes, in the turn to community governance and community responsibility, social problems and social responsibilities are reframed as the duty of the individual and his or her community.[15] In calling the state on its failure to meet its obligation to its young people and on its reframing of youth crime as a social problem to be solved outside of the criminal justice system or prison-industrial complex, young people revealed how the state had withdrawn from its responsibilities. To repeat the words of the activist quoted above, "[We] have been abandoned by the Board of Supervisors and the State of California." Campaign members offered alternative programs to incarceration, such as community-based programs, pretrial reporting centers, and home supervision programs. They also pointed to increasing evidence that youth incarceration and detention does not diminish youth crime or violence, nor does it foster rehabilitation.[16]

Youth of color activists against the Super Jail called attention to the state's desertion of them, best articulated in their challenge to redistribute state resources, or taxpayer money, from incarceration to education. Danny, a Mien AYPAL youth, exposed the state's preference for youth punishment over empowerment when he yelled passionately through a megaphone at a rally outside a meeting of the California Board of Corrections in Sacramento on a sunny day in November 2001: "And California ranks number one in jails and forty-first in education, so why should we go to school? What we want is more money to be spent in schools, not in jails. Locking us up in jails, what will that do? You will take away our futures. You should spend that money on schools instead." Danny was one of approximately sixty AYPAL youth and a hundred others who had opted to skip school to spend a day at the state capital, demanding that the Board of Corrections reject the Alameda County supervisors' proposal for a larger juvenile hall. The large group (including me) had ridden up in a caravan of rented vans to participate in the board's meeting. Yet when we arrived, we were informed that the meeting had been preemptively adjourned in anticipation of the protestors. This did not deter the group from being heard, however, as they held an impromptu rally in the parking lot of the nondescript industrial building where the meeting had been suspended just minutes before. They forced a board member whom they found lingering behind to listen to their speeches and chants and answer their questions.

Youth activists wanted officials to recognize the overwhelming disparity in the distribution of state resources to incarceration versus education, as voiced in Danny's call for "more money to be spent in schools, not in jails." The estimated cost of the new juvenile facility was $176 million, with additional millions needed to maintain the facility each year. Yet according to the National Education Association Rankings and Estimates in 2005, during 2001 to 2002, California ranked thirty-first in per-pupil expenditures and has consistently ranked below the national average in per-pupil spending since the late 1970s.[17] The young activists against the Super Jail first and foremost drew wide attention to this disparity. Hand-lettered signs at numerous rallies and protests read: "$ For Prevention, Not Incarceration!" Another sign that AYPAL youth favored at rallies was made of large black poster paper cut out to look like prison bars. Young people stood behind or stuck their heads through these signs, which had phrases such as "Expand Minds Not Prisons" written on them in bold white letters (see fig. 3.1). Additionally, young people appealed to tax-paying citizens

3.1. Youth at an anti–Super Jail protest.

and voters of Alameda County to invest in education and other social services rather than incarceration. In a campaign activity aimed at garnering
community support, I spent one Saturday afternoon in Oakland with a
group of AYPAL youth informing shoppers at the entrance of a popular
Safeway grocery store about the costs of youth incarceration. Joseph, who
had immigrated from South Korea two years earlier, approached people,
asking them: "Did you know it would cost almost $200 million to lock up
youth and take this money away from education?" On this occasion, as on
others, the young activists repeatedly called attention to the state shirking
its responsibility to invest in education and tried to shame public officials
into devoting more funds to schools.

Danny, Venus, Joseph, and the hundreds of participants working to stop
the Super Jail also made a link between education and incarceration and
the spread of zero-tolerance crime policies to schools, in what is commonly
referred to as the "school to prison pipeline." Erica Meiners sums up the
phenomenon: "Trapped in failing schools that are often physically deterio-
rating, disciplined and moved into juvenile justice systems through violations of punitive zero tolerance policies, failing to pass high-stakes standardized tests and channeled into special education programs, youth of

color are, materially and conceptually, moved from schools to jails."[18] As an example of federal policies that increased criminalization and punishment in the US educational system, the 1994 Gun-Free Schools Act was passed on the premise that it was necessary to control school violence—even though school violence, like the national youth crime rate, had been declining.[19] The act, which required any state receiving federal funds to institute a policy of a mandatory one-year expulsion for any public school student who brought a weapon to school, has been expanded by schools, which have instituted a host of measures against perceived threats to school authority and order. The problem with the act and other zero-tolerance polices is the subjective implementation of such procedures, which overwhelmingly target youth of color. Specifically, as a 2003 report by the Advancement Project and Civil Rights Project details, African Americans have higher rates of suspension and referrals to special education programs and schools and bear an unequal share of classroom disciplinary actions compared to other racial groups.[20]

As politicized youth of color activists, these young people reframed the issue of incarceration, presenting it not as individual cases of youth criminality and delinquency but as an example of state policies and institutional structures of criminalization. Calling on the state to redirect its resources from youth punishment to education, they adopted strategies used by social movements in the second half of the twentieth century that demanded that the state recognize their rights to representation and undertake the redistribution of resources. They challenged the premise that they were criminal because they were youth of color. Their actions exposed the simultaneous state powers of youth control and care. I argued in the previous chapters that marginalized and racialized youth of color's participation in youth organizing programs is based on the presumption that such participation will keep them from becoming "at-risk." But many of these same young people who fought against the Super Jail fit in the category of "at-risk" youth—poor, urban youth of color—and they disputed their position as targets of state control. By asserting the state's responsibility to care for all young people, they evoked the uneven logic of neoliberal governance used to both enable and to punish youth. In this instance, the young activists who were supported by a dense network of nonprofit organizations successfully mobilized to challenge the state's expansion of its capacity to incarcerate young people. To stay the state's hand in youth criminalization and encourage investments in education instead, these activists followed the logic of the state that positions youth empowerment programs as a management strategy against the potential of youth criminality. They succeeded in stopping the Super Jail, but, as I show in the next section, young people's mobilization against the Super Jail also repeated a familiar political strategy of asking the state for cultural representation and redistribution of resources, a strategy that often failed to recognize the state's power to institutionalize and depoliticize their activism—especially in the form of identity politics.

Youth of Color Identity Politics

Although the youth of color identity was a powerful one that challenged state constructions of racialized and criminalized youth of color, such racial identities and categories are intimately tied to state powers to depoliticize and institutionalize young members of minority groups. The concept of a political "youth of color" emerged alongside youth organizing nonprofits in the late 1980s and 1990s as part of the backlash against state policies to criminalize youth of color.[21] This term draws on the familiar moniker of "people of color" established in the wake of Third World movements in the late 1960s.[22] This identity was embedded in a political and economic critique of social and racial inequalities and served to challenge state power. I described in the previous chapter and elsewhere the institutionalization of activism and state incorporation of minority political aims via the expansion of politically neutral nonprofits.[23] In this process, formerly political identities such as "Asian American" have become assimilated to cultural ones, in part by the material consequence of transforming activists' aims into the goals of professionalized nonprofit organizations that favor providing direct services and addressing individual problems rather than challenging structural and power inequalities. This conversion process is not just material but also ideological, mirrored in the construction of Asian Americans as an apolitical model minority and in the embrace of multiculturalism that evades an analysis of power.

The model minority concept posits Asian Americans as a homogeneous racial group that has achieved economic and educational success independent of government aid. They are viewed as subjects without need of state resources and assumed to have no reason for political protest. David

Palumbo-Liu argues that the manipulation of the model minority myth "has had historically profound and far-reaching effects. It has facilitated the splintering off of Asian Americans from progressive political engagement, by working to convince many Asian Americans themselves of their privileged status and the conservative logic that underwrites it, and by aligning Asian Americans with the white middle-class in the eyes of progressive activists of other races."[24] Claire Jean Kim adds, "There seems to be an uncertainty about whether Asian Americans are really 'people of color' and the extent to which they are on the same page politically with Blacks and Latinos."[25] According to the model minority schema, Asian American youth are not considered subjects of state violence and criminalization, especially given popular images of them as high-achieving docile school nerds. In underscoring the processes and effects of youth incarceration and criminalization on "black and brown children" in the Super Jail campaign, some of the campaign activists overlooked the steady rise of juvenile arrest rates among Asian and Pacific Islander youth in the Bay Area. In Alameda County specifically, after African Americans, Samoans and Laotians were the groups with the highest rates of juvenile arrests in 2000. Arrest statistics for Asian and Pacific Islander females had increased between 1991 and 2000 by a dramatic 680 percent, an increase of almost six times that of their African American and Latina counterparts.[26] In San Francisco County, Samoan and Vietnamese male youth have two of the highest arrest rates.[27] While national arrest trends for African American and white youth have declined in the past twenty years, the presence of Asian and Pacific Islander youth in the juvenile justice system has grown substantially.[28]

Marie, an AYPAL staff member who was part of the decision-making team of the campaign to stop the Super Jail, became weary of constantly reminding others in the coalition that youth incarceration had to be analyzed beyond a "black and brown" paradigm to include a more nuanced analysis of race and criminalization. Marie expressed her frustration at how incarceration of Asian and Pacific Islander youth was rendered invisible, even among people in the coalition, and even in spite of the fact that the young people's activism and presence at campaign actions were acknowledged. She told me: "Even though they do have APIs [Asian and Pacific Islanders] involved, they don't talk as much about the Asian experience in juvie [juvenile hall]. And also, like, they'll forget, they'll say it's a black and Latino thing when they are on the radio, which is incorrect." AYPAL youth

3.2. The "Southeast Asian Youth Say No Super Jail" puppet.

and staff also repeatedly pointed to their omission by members in the coalition as well as reporters. Kathy, a Mien youth, spoke to this issue during a focus group interview when the discussion turned to the Super Jail campaign: "Like the media, the newspaper and media—every time they say something about the rallies, they don't usually include AYPAL even though it's most of us out there." To boldly mark their presence and challenge the dominance of a "black and brown" discourse in the campaign, Cambodian members of AYPAL made a large papier-mâché puppet of a young person holding a sign that read "Southeast Asian Youth Say No Super Jail" (see fig. 3.2). The Cambodian youth made the puppet out of frustration at being ignored, but also to highlight the increasing incarceration rates among Cambodian, Laotian, and Mien youth. The ten-foot puppet loomed above the protestors at subsequent campaign actions.

AYPAL's protest against the presentation of youth incarceration as a "black and brown" issue and the persistent visibility of Asian and Pacific Islanders in the campaign against the Super Jail challenged state-produced ideological representations of Asian Americans as the model minority, as well as highlighting the extent of the consequences of a depoliticized Asian American identity. Mainstream assumptions about Asian Americans' questionable allegiance to the political causes of people of color were further exacerbated by the racial politics that unfolded among the Alameda County Board of Supervisors, who had the final say about the juvenile hall expansion. One supervisor, who was Chinese American, became a particular target of campaign activists when she reneged on her promise to vote against a larger facility. Although none of the members of the coalition expressed the view that AYPAL members' politics were aligned with the "switcheroo" of the supervisor, the situation underscored the popular perception that Asian Americans are not closely aligned with other people of color, and it served as a reminder of the very real challenges involved in building multiracial political collaborations.

The common view of Asian American youth as unaffected by criminalization or crime was also reinforced within the Asian American community. For instance, an article featured in *AsianWeek*, one of the oldest and largest English newspapers covering the Asian American community in the Bay Area, quickly glossed over the role of Asian and Pacific Islander youth in the Super Jail campaign and detailed the consequences of youth incarceration on African Americans.[29] One AYPAL staff member pointed to the article's oversight by highlighting the participation of AYPAL youth in the campaign, the frequent harassment of many of its members by police officers, and rising incarceration rates especially among Southeast Asians. His response called attention to the implications of practices of exclusion and articulation of state-enforced racial constructions. This persistence also evokes Dylan Rodriguez's claim that when Asian Americans have implicitly reinforced their identity as the model minority, they have been complicit in the construction of African American and Latino criminality in the rise of the prison-industrial complex.[30]

Moreover, a politics of identification and mobilization around a youth of color identity assumes that racism and white supremacy affect diverse groups of young people in similar ways. Alternatively, Andrea Smith asserts that people of color organizing needs to adopt frameworks that do not assume racism and white supremacy are singular processes but rather are tied to interrelated logics of slavery and capitalism, genocide and capitalism, and Orientalism and war that recognize people of color as both victims of and complicit in white supremacy. This expanded framework, Smith argues, allows for alliances that consider the unique histories of different populations and that are also accountable to each group.[31] Although the campaign to stop the Super Jail was organized around a youth of color identity—a political identity that directly challenged processes of state criminalization and incarceration of youth of color—it was not immune to adopting racial representations of Asian Americans that the state also used. The pervasive construction of Asian Americans as the model minority situated them as outside the reaches of youth incarceration and criminalization. Despite the omission of AYPAL youth by other activists at times during the campaign, their role and participation did not go unnoticed. I was present at an AYPAL meeting one afternoon in December 2001, when one of the members of the Board of Supervisors who generally sided with the activists dropped by unannounced, so that he could "meet and talk with the youth who had been so instrumental in the fight against the Super Jail." His visit was remarkable because none of the young people present were of voting age, nor did he represent the political district where they lived. Campaign literature also was later adjusted to include "Asian and Pacific Islanders" along with "black and brown youth" on "lock-down."

Nevertheless, I argue that this instance of AYPAL youth organizing not only underscores the persistence of identity politics (such as youth of color) and the practices of exclusion that such a politics may prompt, but it also serves as a reminder that we must critically address the way such identifications produce and limit political coalitions and affinities. The role of the state in affirming various identity-based categories must be recognized, as well as the limitations of such identifications in the nation-state's privileging frameworks of race.[32] If indeed "subjects are formed through the work of institutions and discourses," as Inderpal Grewal suggests, then "we need to focus on new assemblages of power."[33] We must account for the differing impacts of neoliberal state powers and the divergent ways that racial minority groups may be advertently or inadvertently complicit in the oppression and negation of the political needs of others. In the following section, I describe how this diverse group of Asian and Pacific Islander youth, with different immigration histories and experiences with racial discrimination, used racial identities as a strategy for political struggle. In particular, I sift through an incident that highlighted the differing experiences of criminalization among AYPAL youth in the fight against the Super Jail. I use this example to illuminate how, as members of a panethnic organization dedicated to social justice, AYPAL youth negotiated, identified, and organized around a different kind of racial politics.

Beyond Multiculturalism

As a group, the young participants of AYPAL had "deep" feelings about the campaign to stop the Super Jail and were proud of their role in it. One youth asserted: "It's the best thing I've done." But there also were divergences of opinions and experiences. As individuals, they felt differently about the process and effects of criminalization on youth of color. They were not in the habit of identifying themselves as youth of color or as Asian and Pacific Islanders on a daily basis. If pressed, they more readily identified with their specific identity as Filipina, Mien, Khmer, or Tongan. These distinctions were most clearly seen in the planning of the Asian and Pacific Islander (API) Institute. The institute is a yearly conference that gathers members of Asian and Pacific Islander youth organizations from across the Bay Area; every year, one youth group takes charge of planning the entire event. In 2002 AYPAL agreed to organize the institute, and the Cambodian and Chinese members of AYPAL volunteered to take the lead. The young people met regularly for a couple of months to plan the conference. At the first planning meeting, three adult staff members—Marie, Penny, and I— gathered with thirteen youth. We sat around a large table in the basement of a community space at the edge of Oakland's Chinatown. The goal of the meeting was to come up with a theme for the API Institute. Penny suggested that young people put forward possible topics of interest for API youth in the Bay Area. The brainstorming produced this list: youth movements, art and activism, youth violence, globalization, criminalization of youth, and health and sex education. A round of voting narrowed the topics to health and sex education and criminalization of youth. This led to an intense debate. Some argued for organizing the institute around the theme of youth criminalization:

Matt: It [criminalization of youth] is relevant to us right now with our work with Books Not Bars and juvie hall campaign. Also youth will be bored with the topic of sex ed because they hear it all the time—at school, from counselors, etc., and it will seem like we are preaching to them and they might rebel at the institute.

Cindy: There's lots of youth in jail just because of the way they look and the colors and stuff.

John: We need to do this because we don't learn about it in school.

Others argued for the topic of health and sex education:

Jenny: [But] there are lots of girls that are pregnant and need to learn about abstinence.

Karen: People need to know about it [sexual education].

Matt and Cindy, two Cambodian American youth, argued most passionately for the topic of youth criminalization, whereas Jenny and Karen, two Chinese American youth, were most vocal in favor of health and sex education. They questioned the notion of youth criminalization. At several points in the meeting, Jenny asked, "What do you mean by criminalization? How are youth criminalized?"

The striking manner in which divisions between the two groups played out in this meeting revealed the differences in the racialization of Asian and Pacific Islander youth within AYPAL and the gendered aspects of youth criminalization. Marie offered an explanation: "Well, I'm not sure, but I mean Cambodians are darker and I don't know if that plays into it [the differences and stereotypes]. Also the different ethnic groups are from different economic backgrounds, so I'm sure that plays into it too." Here, Marie points to the uneven processes of youth criminalization, echoing what Aihwa Ong argues is the differentiated racialization and positioning of Cambodian refugees that does not align with the upwardly mobile model minority.[34] Although the majority of AYPAL youth came from working-class families, differences of class existed among the group. For instance, both Jenny and Karen came from families with stable incomes (Karen's father worked in construction), whereas Cindy and Matt's families depended on part-time work and government assistance. Jenny and Karen were also exceptional students at their schools, supporting stereotypes of Asians as the model minority. Additionally, their questioning of youth criminalization reinforces how the processes of criminalization are often targeted at young men of color. Although young women of color are also targets of criminalization, as shown in Venus's comments above, their regulation is overwhelmingly concentrated on controlling their sexual morality, as Karen and Jenny's remarks indicate.

Despite such different opinions, the AYPAL members chose youth criminalization as the theme for the API Institute and connected it to their organization's efforts against the Super Jail. Karen and Jenny, after attending AYPAL workshops on youth criminalization and learning about the disproportionate number of youth of color in juvenile hall, began to articulate a critique of the political system that was increasing its capacity to lock up youth of color. They became leaders in organizing the institute on youth criminalization and attended rallies alongside their peers in the campaign to halt the Super Jail. What triggered their participation, however, depended more on their commitment to the principles of social justice and social change as outlined in AYPAL than it did on their direct, personal experiences with youth criminalization. The personal negotiation of the effects of youth criminalization by these AYPAL youth and their decision to organize politically against the Super Jail offer an example of collective panethnic organizing that was attentive to differences within the group. In this case, the youth organized and assembled behind a "youth of color" identity as committed members of AYPAL and the youth of color organizing movement of which AYPAL was part.

Such panethnic identity and political activism were continually nurtured and sustained in the daily practices of AYPAL. Race and racial politics were central to the group, and its cultural and political work was reflected in its organizational structure. In the introduction I explained that AYPAL was purposely created to address youth leadership and activism, issues that community leaders saw as missing among services offered to Asian and Pacific Islander youth in Oakland. These leaders were inspired by the activism of the Asian American movement as well as by the emergence of youth of color organizing nonprofits. But instead of creating a new youth organizing nonprofit, the original stakeholders decided that AYPAL should remain attached to six ethnic-specific social service nonprofit organizations, which would serve as a "home base" and create a youth organizing collaborative that was panethnic. In this way, AYPAL was able to mobilize an activist component within nonprofit organizations that were not deliberately political. For instance, Asian Community Mental Health Services, the leading agency that sponsored AYPAL, is a nonprofit organization created in 1974 that provides multilingual social services such as screening, evaluation, and treatment for mental health and substance abuse; counseling; and family services, including therapy, outreach, and case management to address intergenerational conflicts, traumas, and acculturation, among other issues. Likewise, Asian Health Services, formed in 1968, is another nonprofit that provides direct health services to many uninsured or Medicaid patients in Oakland. These organizations are some of the many institutions spearheaded by politically active second-generation Asian American college students and community activists in the wake of the 1960s social movements to establish organizations for its community members. Many of these Asian American nonprofit organizations were explicitly based on the principle of "serve the people and promote revolution" and influenced by the Black Panther Party's "Ten Point Program," which sought to meet basic social services needs as well as promote revolutionary education.[35] Not all of the ethnic nonprofit organizations established in this period were radical in origin, but the commitment to serve the larger pan–Asian American community was central.[36] Yet, as it happens with many ethnic social service organizations, the groups' political aims to serve the people and transform the institutions of care and control have themselves become institutionalized as I have elaborated in chapter 2. I repeat AYPAL's organizational structure and this history of Asian American nonprofits here to recognize the emphasis of race and racial identity in creating ethnic nonprofits as well as the depoliticization of these organizations. I contend that AYPAL's rootedness in established ethnic nonprofit organizations with a youth activist component is an example of an organization that recognizes this past and moves beyond its limitations.[37]

Young people's cultural and racial identities were emphasized through workshops, projects, and cultural arts projects that were designed to connect their cultures with political histories in ways that did not fall into the trap of a "wishy-washy" multiculturalism. Henry, a staff member, explained,

> I really like the way that AYPAL . . . is an organization that is pan-Asian but it was also really clearly defined by ethnic group. I think that other pan-Asian groups tend to like throw all the Asians together in this free-for-all. . . . I tend to think that API groups that just throw everybody together tend to just

mishmash all the issues and then create this kind of wishy-washy diversity that doesn't really hold its own . . . you know? And I feel the same way about . . . different kinds of multiculturalism where people just say we want a multicultural group and they will throw everybody in the room and then they won't do enough to address the particular issues of each group.

In contrast, AYPAL attended to the cultural recognition and representation of the different racial groups present, but not for the purpose of merely "celebrating" diversity.

Rather, differences and similarities among AYPAL members were learned and shared as points of affiliation around political and social struggle. For instance, the Mien youth conducted an oral history project of their elders in their community, who, unlike them, were born and raised in the highlands of Laos. Through the project, the young people learned how Mien men, such as their grandfathers, fathers, and uncles, were recruited by the Central Intelligence Agency (CIA) to fight against the communist forces of the Pathet Lao. When the war ended on the side of the Pathet Lao, many Mien families were forced to flee their country as refugees. One Mien youth said: "It's not just about learning about other people's history, but I learn about my own, too, like some of the stuff I never knew. Like I knew how they [my parents] struggled, but I didn't know how when they came here they had a hard experience and stuff and how the CIA recruit[ed] the Mien people during the war and stuff." In these groups, the importance of young people's specific cultural and racial background was endorsed. But such recognition was centrally tied to a political history. It did not replicate what Jason, an AYPAL staff member, has called the "four F's"—food, fashion, famous people, and festivals—that have come to define politically neutral claims to culture and diversity in this era of multiculturalism. The young people's specific identities as Asian and Pacific Islander or as youth of color were not necessarily celebrations of culture, but rather political affiliations of struggle and collective action.

In this manner, AYPAL's activities rejected liberal notions of multiculturalism as divorced from political analyses of power inequalities, which have encouraged a celebration of cultural diversity rather than an emphasis on cultural parity.[38] Jodi Melamed traces this convergence of neoliberalism and multiculturalism from the 1970s on: "Detached from the history of racial conflict and antiracist struggle, 'culture,' as the displacement of racial reference, nonetheless remains associated with ideas of 'diversity,' 'representation,' and 'fairness.'"³⁹ When articulated through a multicultural logic of equality and inclusion, and through the celebration of ethnic and cultural differences, race and racial inequalities conveniently disappear from the political field through "moderate redistribution and cultural universalism."⁴⁰

In addition to AYPAL youth's organization around a youth of color identity to challenge the state's incarceration of youth of color like them, I witnessed how the group's members deployed race as a political strategy in different political moments. Concurrently with the campaign against the Super Jail, many of the same AYPAL youth banded together as "Asian and Pacific Islanders" to protest the exclusion of Pacific Islanders by Chinese American business and community leaders from the local Asian community center.⁴¹ At numerous community actions and city council meetings, AYPAL youth organized under the banner of Asian and Pacific Islander as a contingent political strategy to express their commitment to diverse and inclusive representation at the cultural center. These identity claims were based not on assertions of authenticity, but on principles of political and social equality. Working against practices of exclusion or fragmentation, these young people's claims to political identity were strategic, issue-based, and informed by political equality. It was a strategy that J. Kehaulani Kauanui describes as "appropriate, *issue-by-issue* in each historical moment."⁴² In a period when race and racial categories had become politically neutral tools of state administration, AYPAL members were able to assert a political racial identification. Although tied to "home" nonprofit organizations that catered more to providing direct services, the youth organizing component of AYPAL managed to maintain its political agenda and assert a panethnic political identity that was defined according to principles of social justice reminiscent of the Asian American movement—despite the institutionalization of Asian American nonprofits by the state.

Chapter 4

CONFRONTING THE STATE

In April 2003, AYPAL youth members visited the local office of their US representative to discuss the issue of Cambodian refugee deportations. They wanted to tell their congresswoman about AYPAL's campaign to put an end to the deportation of documented US residents (such as permanent residents and refugees) who were not citizens. Jason—another adult staff member—and I accompanied the three youth, Alex, Sandy, and Young. Also present were two sisters of Sammy, another AYPAL youth member, who had come to plead on behalf their brother, Boran. Sammy had been born in the United States, but Boran came to this country from Cambodia as a toddler when his family fled the Khmer Rouge. Instead of being released after serving a sentence for a crime he had committed, he was transferred directly to an Immigration and Naturalization Services detention center and slated for deportation to Cambodia. Boran was one of the hundreds of Cambodian refugees whose life course was radically altered by changes in immigration laws, particularly the Illegal Immigration Reform and Immigrant Responsibility Act (IIRIRA) of 1996.

Although the meeting had been scheduled months in advance, in the hope that the congresswoman would meet with the group, an aide represented her instead. The AYPAL youth had carefully prepared for the meeting. Young, a Korean American female, started the meeting by facilitating the introductions and passed out meeting agendas. Sandy, a Chinese American female, tackled the first agenda item and spoke about the injustice of the IIRIRA, which required that noncitizens who had served a prison sentence be deported and consequently broke up families. Boran's two sisters spoke tearfully of how their brother, if he was deported, would leave behind his toddler and pregnant wife, who would then be responsible for raising their family on a single income. Sandy handed the aide a list with the names of over a dozen allies and endorsers of AYPAL's campaign. Last, Alex, a Vietnamese youth, detailed AYPAL's demands, which the three young people had written on a large piece of poster board that they placed on an easel during the meeting. The poster read: "1) We want the congresswoman to sponsor a bill in Congress that would repeal the 1996 IIRIRA"; and "2) We want her to co-sponsor a press conference where she will publicly present her plans to repeal the law and raise awareness in the community about the problem of deportation."

The aide appeared sympathetic and assured the group that the congresswoman disagreed with the IIRIRA. But he warned them of the backlash against immigrants and the conservative climate in Washington, D.C., and the rest of the country in the wake of the attacks of September 11. He outlined the difficulties of repealing existing laws, but he promised to discuss the issue with the congresswoman and to look into developing a "Dear Colleague" letter about the IIRIRA to send to her allies in Congress. He also agreed to host a joint press conference with AYPAL to announce the congresswoman's plan of action against the IIRIRA, although he noted that scheduling difficulties might keep her from attending. He then praised the young people for their active political involvement: "I would like to appreciate your level of activism, especially those of you who are in high school who are at the table. It's refreshing. When I was in high school I can't remember being this active or involved. I didn't even know who my member of Congress was." Immediately following the meeting, everyone was optimistic. The youth were both pleased and relieved to be done with what they thought had been a successful meeting; Sammy's sisters were encouraged by the aide's pledge that the congresswoman's office would look into Boran's situation; and Jason and I were proud of the young people's confidence during the meeting and their ability to persuade the aide to commit to concrete steps to meet each of their demands. Our enthusiasm was short-lived, however. In the month immediately following the meeting, Boran was deported to Cambodia, and it took another year before the congresswoman acted on AYPAL's demands.

This chapter addresses state governance and young people's relationship to the state as political actors. I detail the involvement of AYPAL youth in their campaign to put an end to the deportation of permanent residents and refugees previously convicted of a crime, particularly Cambodian refugees. AYPAL's campaign spanned a period of two years (2002 to 2004) and culminated with their congresswoman's cosponsorship of a bill (H.R. 3309) to repeal the IIRIRA. This law, along with the Anti-Terrorism and Effective Death Penalty Act, made significant changes that facilitated the deportation of "criminal aliens"—noncitizens convicted of crimes including permanent residents and refugees—to their home country after serving a prison sentence. Yet it was the signing of a formal repatriation agreement—a memorandum of understanding—between Cambodia and the United States on March 22, 2002, that instigated the deportation of Cambodian refugees and became a concern for AYPAL. According to the Returnee Integration Support Center in 2010, 229 Cambodians had been deported since 2002.[1] In 2008, a reported 2,000 awaited deportation.[2]

In this campaign, AYPAL youth veered from familiar youth organizing topics of educational justice and youth incarceration to come face to face with state power by tackling a federal immigration policy. Young people directly pressured their representative in the US Congress and engaged in practices that constitute elemental democratic principles. In doing so, they put to the test the popular discourse of young people as valued political actors. But this process also revealed to AYPAL youth not only the limitations of the power of youth in the democratic process but also the confines of a liberal democratic state. After repeated attempts to pressure their congresswoman to meet their demands, they realized that in a representative democracy, they had little power over her because they were not of voting age. Thus, they engaged a state that encouraged them to be active citizens but denied them fundamental access to the state—the right to representation and a voice in their own governance. Yet in confronting the limits of their relationship to the state, AYPAL youth revealed that a neoliberal state that perpetrates daily violence through the practice of expulsion of its undesirable "others" is also an imperial state. Learning of deportation cases around them, the young people came to understand that the discourses and practices of democratic citizenship are produced by the US government, whose political hegemony extends beyond the country's borders. Unable to overturn the IIRIRA, AYPAL youth nonetheless continued to call attention to this immigration policy. They criticized the deportation of refugees like Boran, who not only had served a sentence for his crime but was also forced to return to the country from which the United States had presumably rescued him. AYPAL youth campaign work exposes deportation as a technique used by neoliberal governance to produce desirable citizen-subjects—those who exercise good personal choice and personal responsibility—while rendering invisible the legitimatization of state violence and power. Lastly, the young people's activism and critique speaks to the potential and need for youth of color organizing to address the transnational deployment of US imperial hegemony.

Deportation and Personal Responsibility

President Bill Clinton signed the IIRIRA into law on September 30, 1996. The law and the Anti-Terrorism and Effective Death Penalty Act, passed in April of the same year, have radically altered immigration policies. These laws required and accelerated the expulsion of both documented (such as permanent US residents and refugees) and undocumented immigrants if they had been sentenced to prison or probation for a crime. The two laws changed existing legislation in several key regards. For example, they reduced from five years to one year the required duration of a prison sentence that triggers deportation; they redefined "aggravated felony"; they "grandfathered," or made retroactive, these new prerequisites; and they instituted mandatory detention without bail or due process for all immigrant or refugee defendants facing deportation. Aggravated felony now includes nonserious crimes for which the sentence of incarceration or parole exceeds 365 days, lowering the threshold for crimes eligible for deportation. Violations such as urinating in public, bouncing a check, or failing to pay a subway fare now qualify as causes for deportation. The IIRIRA also denied individuals the right to have their cases reviewed by an immigration judge, so that person could take into consideration the defendant's need to support a family and rehabilitation, as well as the severity of the crime.[3]

The changes made by the 1996 laws are the confluence of several factors: increased vigilance against terrorism after the bombings of the World Trade Center in 1993 and Oklahoma City in 1995; the anti-immigrant backlash revived in the 1990s, as evidenced by the passing of Proposition 187, the "Save Our State Initiative" that directly targeted undocumented citizens' right to publicly funded benefits in California; and Republicans' winning control of both houses of Congress in the November 1994 elections.[4] The IIRIRA was passed a month after the 1996 Personal Responsibility and Work Opportunity Reconciliation Act, also known as the Welfare Reform Act, which drastically cut welfare benefits and replaced them with workfare programs. These laws underscore the central tenets of neoliberalism: privatization and personal responsibility. In including both "immigrant responsibility" and "personal responsibility" in the laws' titles, the government firmly established individuals' claim to state rights from a matter of social policy with public implications to one of personal responsibility and exercise of "good" self-governance. The IIRIRA, for example, legitimized the "criminal alien" as a category deemed morally reprehensible, regardless of the severity of the crime.

As recent scholarship argues, deportation, like immigration, is not only an economic policy that disciplines labor and depresses wages but also is a political instrument of the capitalist neoliberal state.[5] The logic of neoliberal capitalism privatizes citizenship as a self-governing exercise that reproduces a moral political economy, which distinguishes between worthy and unworthy citizens. Based on discourses of immigrant responsibility and governmental efficiency toward the immigration problem, the immigration policies enacted in 1996 are key to the neoliberal regime's effort at disciplining its immigrant population. The detention and removal of supposedly irresponsible noncitizens highlight the forces of surveillance, criminalization, incarceration, and detention of the US empire before September 11, which has been ever more pronounced in the aftermath of that attack. Sunaina Maira notes: "A crucial point is that the 'post 9-11' moment is not a radical historical or political rupture, but rather a moment of renewed contestation over the state's imperial power and ongoing issues of war and repression, citizenship and nationalism, civil rights and immigrant rights."[6] This regime of deportation and detention of immigrants and refugees mandated in the 1996 IIRIRA is also shown in the criminalization and marking of "suspected terrorists" mandated in the 2001 USA PATRIOT Act. It is a racialized regime of punishment and discipline. Just as the processes of criminalization and incarceration overwhelmingly target racial minority groups, Arab, Arab American, Muslim, and South Asian immigrants have been subjects of deportation and detention as part of the US war on terror.[7]

The events of September 11 definitively facilitated the removal of unwanted immigrants—documented and otherwise. The administration of President George W. Bush stepped up its deportation efforts by pursuing repatriation agreements with countries that did not already have official arrangements with the United States. Southeast Asian countries were of particular interest to the United States because, by 2001, one-third of the detainees in Immigration and Naturalization Services detention centers were of Southeast Asian descent.[8] The memorandum of understanding between Cambodia and the United States was a strong-arm tactic on the part of the United States, as it threatened to deny foreign aid to Cambodia and also US visas to Cambodian officials.[9] The United States signed a memorandum of understanding with Vietnam in January 2008 and is seeking a similar agreement with Laos. For Southeast Asian communities, it was not until the signing of the memoranda that the impact and consequences of the IIRIRA fully materialized. No Southeast Asian refugees had been removed to Cambodia and Vietnam since the Vietnam War—not since the US government and people accepted them in an ostensible act of benevolence.[10]

Moreover, although mandatory detention of suspected terrorists has come under scrutiny since the passage of the USA PATRIOT Act, indefinite detention of noncitizens was not uncommon before September 11. For instance, subjects whose countries of origin did not have formal repatriation agreements with the United States were held for undefined periods in Immigration and Naturalization Services detention centers after serving prison sentences.[11] Kim Ho Ma, a Cambodian refugee who fit this profile, spent a year and a half in a detention center and eventually challenged the legality of indefinite detention in 2000.[12] The Supreme Court ruled on his behalf, but Ma was deported, just seven months after the signing of the memorandum of understanding between the United States and Cambodia.[13] Additionally, in 2003 the Supreme Court rejected a due process challenge to mandatory detention without bond made by Hyung Joon Kim, a permanent resident from South Korea. Kim, who immigrated to the United States with his family at the age of six, was deemed deportable after serving a prison term for shoplifting less than $100 worth of merchandise from a local store, his actions falling under the expanded definition of "aggravated felony" of the IIRIRA.[14] The fluid movement of deportees from imprisonment to detention in facilities that also restrain US citizens points to the interlocking mechanism of incarceration and deportation. Deportation enacts a racialized neoliberal regime of punishment (detention, incarceration, and deportation) and governance (shaping good and bad moral subjects). None of the AYPAL youth I worked with had heard of the IIRIRA or the memorandum of understanding with Cambodia until they took on the campaign against deportation. But they knew of the pending deportation of Boran—the brother of Sammy, their fellow AYPAL member—and they directly challenged the state to do something about the case.

"The Wheels of Justice Work Slowly"

With passionate energy, the young people of AYPAL took the task of over-turning the IIRIRA to the one person they believed would meet their demands: the congresswoman who represented their district. In doing so, they pursued a fundamental principle of democracy—the right to fully and equally participate and partake in making decisions about their gover-nance.[15] They spoke with a handful of Bay Area elected officials (or, more precisely, the officials' aides); staged multiple community awareness ac-tions, including several "No Deportation Zone" block parties; held two press conferences; took to the streets in protest; disseminated a report about deportation; and built coalitions with local and national immigrant rights groups and labor unions. In these activities, which comprise the core of liberal democratic politics, the young people embodied in practice the understood characteristics of good US citizenship. They lived up to dis-courses of an active and engaged citizenry and reinforced ideal notions of youth as future leaders of our nation-state. But the majority of AYPAL youth—who were under eighteen years of age—quickly came to realize that within the actual system of representative democracy, they had little clout. In working with their congresswoman, they experienced firsthand "the system" as an institutional bureaucracy made up of formal procedures and policies that narrowly defined political practices.

The young people's first taste of the limits of a representative democracy came when AYPAL staged the first of two press conferences drawing atten-tion to the deportation of Cambodian refugees in May 2003. Approx-imately one hundred people gathered on a cold, windy afternoon in front of the federal building where the congresswoman had her office. They huddled in small circles in the shadow of the building, with its distinctive twin towers joined by an enclosed bridge. The crowd—AYPAL members, associates from its allied organizations, and a few inquisitive bystanders—were expecting to hear the congresswoman announce to the media and the public her plans to repeal the IIRIRA. The youth believed the congress-woman would recognize their months of hard work in her announcement. Instead, they heard from her aide:

> You should know that [the] congresswoman stands in solidarity with you. We absolutely support what you're trying to do. We are absolutely going to try to

repeal the 1996 IIRIRA Act and we're going to try to fight these injustices. . . . We are here today and together we can make a change, we can make a difference. Together we will make a difference. Although sometimes the wheels of justice work slowly, they indeed do move forward and we will put this together to bring it back down. [The] congresswoman will certainly do everything she has in her power to support the bringing down of this act and will encourage her colleagues to bring down this 1996 IIRIRA Act.

Although the aide expressed the congresswoman's support for AYPAL's efforts, it was clear that she had no concrete plan to repeal the IIRIRA. To make matters worse, hardly any representatives of the media were present at the press conference. There were two reporters from local Korean newspapers, but no mainstream television or newspaper reporters. Considering that the major goals of the press conference were to make the congresswoman publicly announce to the media her plans to repeal the IIRIRA and to generate attention about deportation, the event was a failure.

In subsequent meetings during the summer and fall of 2003, AYPAL members reflected on the strengths and weaknesses of the campaign against deportation. At one of these meetings in September, they concluded that AYPAL was rich in "youth power," but it was obvious that a strong youth base was not sufficient to make a congresswoman take notice, let alone change a national immigration policy. They decided that the only way a group of youth might pressure their representative was to garner the backing of the people she was most accountable to—her adult voting constituents. AYPAL's strategy for the following year was twofold. First, youth aimed to exercise grassroots power by building a mass base of community support and raising awareness about the issue of deportation. Second, they planned to use the media to gain moral power in the campaign by alerting the public to the personal stories of deportees and families destroyed by deportation. To achieve these goals, AYPAL youth built a wider coalitional base that extended their network beyond familiar youth organizations. Their labor was evident at an AYPAL "Jedi meeting"—one that gathered youth from all six sites—a little over a year after their first press conference. Marie, a staff member, read from an accomplishment list written with red marker on a large sheet of white paper tacked on the wall:

> —Collected 1,900 signed postcards against deportation and turned it into [the congresswoman].

—Received 60 endorsement forms from local and national organizational
allies.

—Brought out 350 people to the first community block party against deportation.

—Brought out 375 people to the second community block party against
deportation.

—Gathered 400 people to the press conference against deportation.

—Produced a report about deportation.

—Outreached to 14 churches, unions, and other community organizations.

The list encapsulated the countless hours on both weekdays and weekends
that everyone at the meeting had spent on the campaign. This was in
addition to AYPAL's membership in the Southeast Asian Freedom Network, a national coalition of grassroots organizations working to put an
end to refugee deportations. The coalition had been formed in 2002 to
respond to the sudden mandate of Cambodian deportation put into devastating effect just months after the signing of the memorandum of understanding. The group sought to provide aid to those facing removal and to
create a national network of activists working to prevent their deportation.

In another attempt to pressure their congresswoman to support a bill
that would repeal the IIRIRA, AYPAL youth staged a second press conference almost a year after their first one. This time, three television reporters (from ABC's Channel 7, KTVU's Channel 2, and UniVision), their
cameramen, and newspaper reporters from the *San Francisco Chronicle*
and the *Contra Costa Times* attended. The youth had spent the past year
increasing their access to the press by forming a youth media production
team and partnering with the Youth Media Council, a Bay Area organization dedicated to developing youth-led strategies for media justice. Additionally, to gain moral power, AYPAL had produced a report called *Justice
Detained: The Effects of Deportation on Immigrant Families*, which described the impact of the IIRIRA with detailed statistical findings and
personal stories of deportees and their family members. Youth interns
interviewed the deportees and their relatives; the Data Center, a think tank
research center that provides campaign research to social justice organizers, helped analyze the data; and AYPAL staff authored the report. It was
distributed to the press as well as to community members.

But despite building community support and attracting media attention to the campaign, AYPAL still received no indication from the congress-woman's office that she would introduce a law to repeal the IIRIRA. In fact, she did not attend the second press conference, and her aide made no commitments on her behalf about proposing an anti-deportation bill. He repeated the now-familiar refrain: yes, she opposes the law, and we applaud your efforts. But this time, the aide's tone was different:

> I'm here today to tell you that the congresswoman fully supports what you are here for. We fully support the repeal of this terrible, terrible law and we will do everything we can to make sure that this law is repealed, but we need your help. We need you to not be here in front of [the] congresswoman's [office]. She's with you. We need you to be in your communities where they don't understand this issue is on the ballot. We need you to go talk to your friends, your family, and continue to build grassroots coalitions, build the energy, build the momentum, [so] we can get this law repealed. Once the Democrats take over Congress, once we get George Bush out of the White House, we can definitely make it happen, and I want you to know—I want to thank you on behalf of the congresswoman for your support, and thank you for your continued energy and passion.

Yet spreading the word to their friends, family, and community members and building grassroots coalitions were exactly what AYPAL youth had been up to for the past year. And who else had the power to help their cause of repealing a law, if not their congresswoman?

The youth and staff of AYPAL were equally frustrated with their inability to persuade their representative and with the bureaucratic web of represen-tational democracy. The congresswoman's aide chalked up her lack of response to the larger political climate and, more importantly, redirected responsibility onto young people by suggesting that they work harder. In this manner, he articulated neoliberal demands of governance that frame social problems as individual or community problems, in which political change hinges on the individual's—or, in this case, young people's—"help." The aide also reinforced the idea of citizenship and politics as matters of personal choice and practice. But AYPAL members were tired of hearing him make vague promises on behalf of the congresswoman at press con-ferences two years in a row. Everyone also was losing steam at this juncture of the campaign. What was their next step, and what did they need to do to persuade the congresswoman? These were the main questions at hand during an emergency Jedi meeting in April 2004. All they had scheduled was another confirmed meeting with the congresswoman, but no one was convinced that she would actually face the group, let alone agree to introduce a bill to repeal the IIRIRA. Ideas included such entertaining ones as asking Oprah Winfrey to do a special television show on deportation, as well as more sensible ones, like holding a community town-hall meeting with the congresswoman, and increasing media exposure. But one thing was clear—they needed to escalate their activities to force her to take action. They ultimately decided to return to their original demands: a meeting at which the congresswoman would actually be present and commit to introducing a bill in Congress to repeal the IIRIRA, and a public event during which she would be held accountable to AYPAL's demands.

Doing last-minute online research the day before their scheduled meeting with the congresswoman, an AYPAL staff member made an unexpected discovery. He learned that a bill to repeal the IIRIRA (H.R. 3309) had been introduced in Congress by a representative from San Diego in October 2003. The bill proposed exactly what AYPAL members demanded: "to amend the Immigration and Nationality Act to restore certain provisions relating to the definition of aggravated felony and other provisions as they were before the enactment of the Illegal Immigration Reform and Immigrant Responsibility Act of 1996." The news came as a shock. In a scramble of last-minute phone calls, e-mails, and meetings, AYPAL youth deliberated their next campaign steps and, more immediately, how to proceed at the meeting the next day with the congresswoman. They decided that the demands they would bring to her at the meeting were: to cosponsor H.R. 3309 instead of proposing a new bill, to write a "Dear Colleague" letter in support of the bill, to write a press release about her support of the bill, and to speak at an AYPAL event to recognize the group's efforts.

The next day at the meeting, the youth once again faced not the congresswoman, but her aide. He expressed enthusiasm at the idea of her cosponsorship of the bill, but he warned the young people to prepare for a long, uphill battle in their attempt to repeal the IIRIRA. They were not dismayed. Jun, a Korean American, replied: "I'll wait till I am old and gray if I have to, to see the IIRIRA repealed." "I'm not discouraged by how long it'll take, it only makes me want to fight harder," added Michelle, a Cambodian American. The congresswoman officially cosponsored the bill four months later. Not surprisingly, H.R. 3309 died in Congress, and no attempt has been made to reintroduce it. There is no indication that the IIRIRA will be repealed despite the claim of the congresswoman's aide that it could be under the leadership of a Democratic president. Rather, deportation of criminal aliens has hit an "all-time high" in 2011 according to the Office of Immigration Statistics.[16] Moreover, recent activism has brought light to the fact that in 2011, 22 percent of deportees had children who were US citizens. When their parents are detained and deported, these children are placed in foster care, further disrupting family ties. By a conservative count, approximately 5,100 of such displaced children were in foster care in 2011.[17]

In the end, AYPAL members never met face to face with the congresswoman. The young people had decided to present her with an award to entice her to meet with them in person, and also maintain amicable ties with her office, but the closest contact they ever had with her was via a previously recorded video message she sent to the group, in which she stated: "I want to take the opportunity to thank all my friends at AYPAL for all the hard work and awareness you have brought to our community regarding the inherent unfairness that has been the result of the 1996 Illegal Immigration Reform and Immigrant Responsibility Act." A representative from her office aired it during an end-of-the-school-year event, the AYPAL May Arts Festival, but many youth felt the video was impersonal, and it did not receive much attention. The young people were not completely discouraged, however. In the two years of organizing, building coalitions with other organizations, and persistent contacts with the congresswoman's office, a group of teenagers brought to her attention an issue that had not been on her political agenda. Yet the congresswoman's elusiveness underscores the reality of an institutional democracy. As the young people discovered, democracy is not an open practice but is composed of formal representation and bureaucracy in which voters are privileged. The congresswoman's aide had rationalized that "the wheels of justice work slowly," if at all. During their involvement to stop deportation, young people did not experience democracy, but instead the failures of citizenship in more ways than one. Youth may be cherished and promoted as future political leaders, as the rhetoric of democracy often does, but in exercising their political power in the present moment, these young people were cast outside the political process. They were unable to realize citizenship as a political activity or as a right, and they were excluded from participating as full and equal members in society, not unlike the deportees they championed.[18] Although they engaged in citizenship as a political activity, their political practices were not granted the same legitimacy as those of voting adults.

The efforts of AYPAL youth highlight the contradiction of young people's relationship to the state. However unintentional, the failure by the state and its representatives to recognize these young people as actual—rather than merely future—political actors in confronting power restricts the projected aims of youth of color organizing as a progressive social justice movement, especially given that most of its participants are under voting age, still in high school, and introduced to youth organizing as a regulated after-school activity. It shows how the project of youth of color organizing is realized as an affirmative process of governmentality, designed to train young people to become particular kinds of citizen-subjects—self-empowered and responsible for community problems—at the site of the nonprofit. In this case, the power of youth organizing rests more in young people's ideological configuration as good political actors and less in the actual practices and effects of their actions within state-sanctioned routes. Notwithstanding this fact, in the next section, I show how young people confronted the shortcomings of "the system"—the institutional process of engaging in the democratic process—and exposed the liberal democratic state and its production of morally responsible citizen-subjects that rendered invisible the violence of the US imperial regime. While engaging in political practices with the state, they also expressed forms of "dissenting citizenship" that Maira notes "could not conform to ideas of what critiques of the state should look like from a traditional activist or liberal-democratic perspective."[19]

Cambodian Deportees

As they worked on the campaign, AYPAL youth learned of and heard more stories about Cambodian refugees removed or facing expatriation. Probably the most familiar stories of Cambodian refugees affected by the changes in the law are those of Loeun Lun, Many Uch, and Kim Ho Ma, whose stories were featured in *Sentenced Home*, a 2006 documentary directed by David Grabias and Nicole Newnham, and in Deborah Sontag's 2003 article in the *New York Times Magazine*.[20] Lun is a Cambodian refugee who was a baby when his mother fled the Khmer Rouge killing fields; he grew up in an urban housing project in Tacoma, Washington. When he was a teenager, Lun shot a gun into the air at a shopping mall while fleeing from a group of armed boys. Fortunately, no bodily harm was inflicted. He served an eleven-month prison sentence for assault charges. He did his best to put his past behind him. He found gainful employment, married, and had two daughters. On the urging of his Cambodian American wife, who was born in the United States, he applied for US citizenship. When he appeared for his naturalization interview, instead of being allowed to take his citizenship test, he was arrested. It did not matter that the unfortunate incident at the mall had occurred seven years earlier and that he had served his sentence. He was deported three months later, caught up in the retroactive clause of the IIRIRA and the repatriation agreement that mandated his removal to Cambodia.

The issue that concerned the young people of AYPAL most about the plight of deported refugees such as Lun and Boran was the state's disposal of Cambodian refugees as unwanted criminal aliens without taking their full stories into consideration. Foremost among the missing information were the facts of the social and political context of these men's lives. For example, take Uch, awaiting deportation for driving the getaway car at a robbery of a rival gang member's house. He said of his experiences growing up in the housing projects in the Seattle area: "We were a bunch of poor Cambodian, Vietnamese and Laotian kids, hanging around without much adults."[21] He also said: "We wanted to make a name for ourselves, we wanted to be the toughest ones in all of Seattle. The cops called it a gang, but when we grew up we just think we had a bond."[22] Uch's words echo a familiar narrative of surveillance and criminalization heard in stories of other young men expelled or awaiting removal to Cambodia. The linking of the processes of youth of color criminalization and incarceration, particularly of young men, was not new to many AYPAL youth, especially in light of their activism against the Super Jail. (All but two of the Cambodian deportees have been male.) But now they realized the injustice of deportation was added to this process. This point was made clear to the attendees at a conference that AYPAL youth organized in March 2003 to raise community awareness about Cambodian deportation, during which they heard from affected family members. One person said about her brother, then slated for removal: "He will be sent back to Cambodia, but he doesn't know Cambodian culture. He doesn't even know American culture, all he knows is American jails." Another woman at the conference described the inhumane conditions of filth and inadequate health care at the Immigration and Naturalization Services detention center where her brother was being held, awaiting deportation for a crime he had committed ten years prior. She said: "A little package [of Tylenol] costs him three bucks . . . he gets sick all the time . . . and the phone calls—it cost four bucks a minute, you know. This system, they're not only detaining people, but they're making a profit off of them. And it ain't right!" These examples illustrate the interlocking regimes of criminalization, deportation, and the prison-industrial complex. With the added step of deportation, youth now understood that the US state powers of criminalization and imprisonment were not limited by its borders.

Sammy, whose brother had been expatriated, spoke out against incarceration and deportation in an unpublished op-ed piece he wrote to a local newspaper and shared with me: "Most of the time, the deportee has already paid their debt to society, but still they received orders of removal. I believe that people should be punished for actions they did that were wrong. But after they already served their time, then they want to punish them again by deporting them is messed up. Think about what the individual is going through yet alone, [without] his or her family and friends. It is hard to understand how a nation that once welcomed immigrants would send them right back to the war, poverty, and other hardships that they once fled from. In the end, I hope the situation turns out in favor of the immigrants." Cindy, a Cambodian American, also spoke out against the injustice of the removals in a fiery speech at an anti-deportation rally:

> Deportation is not right! And what they are doing to us is that they are not giving us no free trials. And what they are doing to us is double jeopardy. It's like punishing us for a crime we already served, twice. And that is not fair. And they treat immigrants like animals and not humans, giving them no rights, no lawyers, no kind of respect. They treat us like we are unwanted people. But we were also here. We're the ones that made this place what it is. We lived here for most of our lives, half of our lives. And if we're sent back, what the hell are we going to do? What kind of shit do we know there? Like, how are we going to survive? What kind of language is there for us or stuff like that? If they send us back, we ain't got no rights there either.

Although refugee deportation technically does not violate the Fifth Amendment's protection against double jeopardy—being tried for the same crime twice—many deportees and their allies saw little difference between that and the double punishment of incarceration in the United States and lifetime banishment to Cambodia.

Sammy and Cindy underscore that an account of the removal of Cambodians must also take into consideration the story of how they came to the United States as refugees and the part about US intervention in Southeast Asia. Removal of Cambodian refugees, who grew up as Americans, to a country with such a volatile and violent past seemed more than unfair; refugees are not voluntary immigrants, after all—they are the displaced victims of war. In deportation, they are exiled to a country whose government committed genocide against its own people. Having spent almost all of their lives in the United States, they lack the language skills and cultural knowledge to enter, let alone start fresh in, their foreign "homelands." High rates of poverty and unemployment in Cambodia make reentry and adjustment extremely difficult. Deportees are also viewed as outsiders by Cambodian society, and little support exists for deportees there except for one halfway house run by the Returnee Assistance Program (now the Returnee Integration Support Center) in Phnom Penh. After arriving in Cambodia, these deportees are immediately processed and housed in Cambodian prisons before they are allowed to enter society. They report suffering from depression as they confront the reality of never returning to their real homes again; their only option for returning to their family members in the United States under current law is as a corpse in a casket. Moreover, some Cambodians view these deportees as unwanted and unproductive in their society.[23] In a different context, Elana Zilberg reveals the difficulties faced by young El Salvadorian men, who also grew up in the United States and were deported after serving a prison sentence. Beyond personal readjustment, these young people are caught up in zero-tolerance policies imported from the United States and enforced by the El Salvadorian government on returned men who have been marked as gang members.[24] In focusing on the plight of Cambodian refugees, AYPAL members forced a public dialogue about the social conditions of Cambodian criminal aliens as political refugees that revealed the practices of imperial statecraft in disposing of unwanted populations.

Some Cambodian, Laotian, and Mien youth grew up hearing their parents' stories about the methods and consequences of war—violence, rape, torture, murder, starvation, sickness, and suffering—that ravaged their homelands and families during the wars in Southeast Asia. The atrocities of the Khmer Rouge are harrowing. The forces of the Khmer Rouge, led by Pol Pot between 1975 and 1979, sought to turn Cambodia into an agrarian utopia, a goal that left an estimated two million people dead.[25] The Khmer Rouge persecuted many members of the elite and educated classes while forcing thousands of others to work in brutal labor camps. Common stories that have surfaced about this time include descriptions of tortured and maimed bodies left for dead on stakes or buried alive, and the infamous killing fields. It is no surprise that parents who lived through the Cambodian genocide find orders to deport their sons unbearable and unfathomable. Paularita Seng, president of the Cambodian Women's Association in Seattle, observed: "The deportations really rattle these mothers, more than Americans could possibly imagine. . . . During the Khmer Rouge time, the soldiers would take away their sons and their husbands for 're-education,' and they knew it was a death sentence. Now, once again, the authorities are at the door for their men."[26] Her comment reinforces the process of criminalization and punishment that mark young men of color and leaves women of color—mothers, sisters, and partners—with the collateral damage of deportation.

The expulsion of Cambodian refugees as a rightful return of criminals to a country ravaged by civil war fails to acknowledge the direct role and impact of US policies on the plight of Cambodian refugees. First, US bombings along the Cambodian border during the Vietnam War not only displaced thousands of people but also reduced the country's economic infrastructure and agricultural productivity to shambles.[27] Second, the inadequacy of the US government policies to resettle displaced Southeast Asian groups has shaped the welfare of these communities.[28] The temporary Interagency Task Force, created by President Gerald Ford in 1975 to deal with the sudden influx of Southeast Asian refugees, quickly proved unsuccessful. The task force acknowledged its botched attempts to swiftly assimilate refugees and minimize their economic impact on local communities by dispersing them across the United States through family sponsorships.[29] Lavinia Limon, the executive director of the US Committee for Refugees, states: "The Cambodians are manifestly the greatest failure of the refugee program in this country. . . . Mistake No. 1 was that we didn't treat the Cambodians as different. The scope and breadth and depth of what they endured—the only thing you can compare it to, was the Jewish Holocaust."[30] Moreover, the majority of Cambodian refugees who survived the Khmer Rouge were often poor and less educated, and they came from rural areas and were hardly prepared for urban life. A recent survey in Los Angeles County, home to the largest Cambodian community in the United States, revealed that Cambodians rank the highest in most indicators of social poverty, including income and education levels.[31] In Oakland, almost half the Cambodian population lived below the poverty line, according to the 2000 Census.[32]

The children of these refugees such as Boran, Lun, Ma, and Uch do not fit the mold of sensationalized news stories of successful, middle-class Asian American students idealized in the model minority myth. The men featured in the film *Sentenced Home*, like Boran, left Cambodia as infants and grew up on the streets of Seattle and Oakland, where they were caught up in a system of crime as well as a system of criminalization that targets youth of color. They were child refugees who fled because of war in their country, and the US government was involved in their displacement and resettlement. The social, political, and economic context of Cambodian refugees constitutes a wider framework in which to situate the lives of these men and their deportations. Yet, in ignoring these larger circumstances surrounding their plight, their removal is justified within the neoliberal logic of expelling "bad" criminals who failed to exercise self-responsibility. Deportation is enforced as a consequence of individual moral irresponsibility or criminal behavior. This policy fails to recognize the ruthless exercise of the state's power in controlling unwanted immigrant populations.

By widening the story of deportation from its narrow focus on the individual refugee criminal, AYPAL youth countered these regimes of state control. Consider, for instance, the young people's critique I witnessed at an AYPAL meeting late one afternoon. About fifteen youth—largely Cambodian and Mien—who were responsible for the logistics of the upcoming first press conference on deportation were gathered around a long wooden table to plan for the event. Marie, who was facilitating the session with me, reminded the group that this was a press event and that we should think of some powerful images or symbols to grab the media's attention. Johnny suggested: "We should play on this theme about deportation hurting families." The other young people nodded their heads in response. Matt excitedly suggested: "We could paint a family portrait and the father's face can be missing, and we'll put a large question mark where his face is supposed to be." "We could write over his face, 'Where is my daddy?'" said Annie. Further underscoring the gendered aspect of deportation, Fay added: "And the child in the picture can have a real sad face on him."

The excitement began to build as others in the room proposed more ideas. Suggestions included a reworking of old recruitment posters showing Uncle Sam, with the saying "I want you!" replaced with "You're next!" Yet everyone was most enthusiastic about Matt's image of the Statue of Liberty. He explained that the statue, instead of representing freedom and liberty for immigrants, should rather stand for "what is really going on with our government." Others jumped on his idea and suggested that boats filled with people being forced back to Asia should be drawn underneath the statue's feet. And in her arm, she would hold a book titled "List of Deportees" with the names of actual deportees written on it. Her other arm would be outstretched, with one finger pointed toward a map of Asia. The Statue of Liberty became a basis of a flier for the press conference (fig. 4.1). Another youth offered a variation on the Statue of Liberty idea, picturing the statue as pulling the Golden Gate Bridge like an elastic slingshot, loaded with those being deported, across a map of the United States and aimed at Asia. The images that young people articulated at this meeting vividly illustrate the critical understanding they have of US imperial statecraft. The Statue of Liberty here is not the gleaming symbol of democracy and freedom but rather a figure that deports "the huddled masses yearning to be free." Deportation is viewed in this instance as a political instrument of state power, repression, and violence. The young people's rendering of the Statue of Liberty takes issue with American exceptionalism and finds irony in the discourse of the United States being made by immigrants and made special because of its immigrants. Their perspective is further exemplified in a chant recited at anti-deportation block parties and rallies:

You wage war on my country,
Now I'm called a refugee.
We are here with our demands,
Join us now and take a stand.
Deportation is a crime,
When we already did our time.
Immigrants are not to blame,
George Bush should be ashamed!

4.1. Sketch of the Statue of Liberty, which became the
basis of a flier for an anti-deportation press conference.
Courtesy of AYPAL.

The chant underscores the state's ruthless punishment ("deportation is a crime, when we already did our time") and calls attention to past and present imperial interventions of US empire ("you wage war on my country, now I'm called a refugee"). By shifting blame from individual immigrants to state power in the chant, the youth criticize a regime that proposes self-responsibility and recognize that policies regarding their welfare are and have always been an apparatus of state expansion and repression.

Exercising Community Power and Building Political Coalitions

As a diverse group whose members come from immigrant and refugee Cambodian, Chinese, Filipino, Korean, Laotian, Mien, Samoan, Tongan, and Vietnamese backgrounds, the consequences of forced removal highlighted the relevance of deportation in AYPAL youth's lives and for their families. Their critique of deportation illuminated how the practices of neoliberal state spanned international borders and it made clear that activism must respond to that fact. It also emphasized the transnational nature of these young people's lives. Quite a number of them had family members living abroad. It was not uncommon to learn that the Mien and Cambodian youth had older siblings or a parent who had stayed behind in Cambodia, Laos, or Thailand in the aftermath of war. Venus, a young Filipina, lived in Oakland with her sister and mother while her father stayed in the Philippines; they visited him occasionally. Others frequently traveled to visit family members abroad or spent part of the year there. For example, CiCi, a Tongan youth, was born in New Zealand and went back there every summer to be with her extended family.

The campaign gave many young people the opportunity to connect with their parents and other family members in new, meaningful ways. For example, the Cambodian youth produced and acted in a play about the Khmer Rouge for their cultural arts project. The play was based on Loung Ung's memoir *First They Killed My Father: A Daughter of Cambodia Remembers*, which recounts how her family survived the Khmer Rouge atrocities.[33] As they learned their lines for the play and in workshops on Cambodian political history, the hardships and violence of their parents' experiences unfolded before them. Pim, a cast member, said she had learned about what her mother "went through, how she survived, and how she worked so hard, and the sacrifices she made. I was born in a refugee camp and now I know what that means. So now I have a lot more respect for her." The play is one example of a different kind of cultural arts project vital to AYPAL, one that allows young people to explore their cultural heritage, the political history of their homeland, and the meanings of racial identity in ways that deviate from the dominant rhetoric of multiculturalism and identity affirmation. The overlap of the play and the campaign offered not only the Cambodian youth but also others the chance to talk with their parents about the past and current situation of their lives. On the flip side, parents and family members showed an interest in the campaign against deportation. On more than one instance, staff members commented on the large number of parents who had come out in support at anti-deportation campaign events, in contrast to other AYPAL campaigns. Sandy, a Chinese ethnic youth whose parents had fled Vietnam as refugees after the war, told me in a personal interview that her parents were impressed with her active role in the visit to the congresswoman's office. Other young people reported that their parents felt proud they were "doing something to help the community."

The most vocal youth during the campaign were, unsurprisingly, Cambodian Americans who readily identified with deportations. The Mien youth, whose parents were also refugees and whose plight was a direct consequence of the US intervention in Laos, were also quite sympathetic to the cause. But other AYPAL youth often shared stories that they had heard at home about family members or family friends who were affected by deportations. They were also aware of and spoke out against the pending deportation of a Bay Area Filipino family, the Cuevas, during the campaign. The Cuevas family, whose three grown children had spent almost their entire lives in the United States, had applied for permanent residence status after overstaying their visa just two weeks after IIRIRA was enacted. Before the 1996 legislation, their situation would have received an individual review that would have taken into account their good moral character and seven continuous years of US residency. They were not afforded this opportunity and were deported in June 2004. Yet AYPAL members' commitment to the campaign was not uniform. A Tongan youth, who acted as spokesperson for the campaign, confided to me in an interview about the anti-deportation campaign: "I just wasn't feeling it at all." Her opinion was informed as much by the lack of response from the congresswoman as it was about the issue at hand. Nonetheless, as a whole, AYPAL youth articulated a unified opposition to deportation.

Unlike their previous campaigns for school reform or against juvenile incarceration, which were youth-centered, these young people recognized deportation as an issue that affected all immigrants—citizens and noncitizens—and their families and communities. In this campaign, the youth formed broader coalitions with immigrant rights groups and adult activists and built multiracial and intergenerational ties. On two different occasions in 2004, youth organized a block party to raise awareness of the issue of deportation in their communities. These events were held in two different Oakland neighborhoods that AYPAL youth marked with "No Deportation Zone" signs. Their hope was to draw as much support from neighborhood residents as possible. The block parties included traditional cultural dances as well as hip-hop performances, games, and arts and crafts booths for children. These festivities supplemented the educational outreach against deportation made in the form of speeches by AYPAL youth and local community activists. The first block party was held at Fruitvale Village in what is known as the San Antonio–Fruitvale neighborhood, which has a high concentration of Southeast Asian and Latino/a residents. The event drew over a hundred people, including AYPAL youth, their friends, families, supporters from various nonprofit organizations, and Latino/a community members. Recognizing the impact of deportation on this community, the youth asked Leo, a youth activist fluent in Spanish as well as English whom they knew from an allied organization, to speak at the event. Mexico was the leading country of origin of persons deported in the United States in 2004, followed by Guatemala and Honduras.[34] The network of immigrant community support that AYPAL youth created at these block parties was in addition to the coalitions they built with immigrant organizations.

Young people's activities against deportation and their critique of the neoliberal state as imperial reveal the fact that deportation is linked to a racialized regime of criminalization and incarceration that extends beyond the US borders. Their activism was confined to the structures and bureaucracy of the United States, but I argue that organizing against deportation forces an analysis of state power as reaching beyond the limits of the nation-state.[35] Monisha Das Gupta's study of advocacy among seven South Asian American nonprofits suggests that it might be more useful to conceive of immigrant rights as transnational and mobile and not bound to national membership, thus reconfiguring rights for immigrants as immigrants and not as citizens.[36] In struggling against Cambodian refugee deportation, AYPAL youth encountered and participated in a larger network led by Asian and Pacific Islander activists that directly confronted state power. As mentioned above, AYPAL was a member of the Southeast Asian Freedom Network, a national coalition of organizations working against Cambodian refugee deportation; the network argued that such removals were intricately tied to the US war on terror. More locally, AYPAL worked with Asians and Pacific Islanders for Community Empowerment (APIforCE), a community organization in Oakland that was deeply involved in the cause of Cambodian deportees. Members of AYPAL were familiar with the political organizing work of other Asian and Pacific Islander activist groups in the Bay Area, such as APIforCE, the Asian and Pacific Islander Coalition against War, and the Filipinos for Global Justice Not War Coalition. Some of these groups were formed in the wake of the events of September 11 and the subsequent deployment of US armed forces to Iraq. For instance, the Filipino coalition was a response to backlash against Filipino immigrants, particularly airport screeners after September 11 (75 percent of all airport screeners in the Bay Area were Filipino). Robyn Rodriguez and Nerissa Balce describe this coalition as an example of "radical Filipino communities that offer an alternative to this problematic US patriotism and Philippine nationalism."[37] These groups not only underscored how various Asian and Pacific Islander communities have been displaced and affected by wars and the US government's role in those wars, but they also called attention to the impact of continued racism in the United States and the vulnerable position of its immigrant populations.

Moreover, these groups connected their activist work to the racial profiling, detention, and deportation of Arabs, Arab Americans, Muslims, and South Asians, as well as to the cause for Palestinians' right to a state of their own. Nadine Naber has documented the ways that the post–September 11 era has opened up new spaces for multiracial coalition building and political critique within communities of color, particularly among Asian Americans and Arab Americans.[38] Asian and Pacific Islander organizations in the Bay Area have been at the forefront of such multiracial coalition building and political activism. This was most visible at the marches against the wars in Afghanistan and Iraq. At the front lines and chanting as part of the people's choir were many representatives of a large network of Asian and Pacific Islander groups, including AYPAL youth, singing in unison against US imperial forces in the Middle East as well as across Asia and the Pacific. Such examples offer glimpses of an activism—both inside and outside of communities of color—that does not privilege institutionalized state racial identities and US borders of organizing that AYPAL youth faced in the campaign against the Super Jail. These various actions and actors point to the need for activism to directly confront power at what Inderpal Grewal refers to as its "transnational connectivities."[39]

In tackling the issue of Cambodian refugee deportation, AYPAL's actions called attention to the governance and construction of immigrants and refugees as good moral neoliberal subjects. By expanding the discussion about deportation as a state violence, they questioned the notion that people like Boran, a criminal and refugee, are bad immigrants who deserve removal. They expressed a sophisticated critique of the imperial state that so relentlessly exercised its powers of exclusion. They articulated the state's irresponsibility toward refugees by pointing out that deportation is a crime, especially because it strips away the liberal rights of due process and legal representation that are an integral part of US democracy. Their actions supported the alternative vision of democracy offered by Wendy Brown, who wrote that "democracy signifies not merely elections, rights, or free enterprise but a way of constituting and thus distributing political power."[40] They challenged discourses of US exceptionalism as a site and bearer of democracy, as suggested by one of my favorite slogans that the youth came up with during the anti-deportation campaign: "Green Card. Accepted Everywhere But Here," a play on the popular MasterCard commercials.

Young people in AYPAL exposed the state and its enthusiastic promotion of youth as future political actors. When they actually engaged the state in the political process in the present moment, they encountered the state's inability to identify and treat them as political actors. This confrontation, I argue, once again renders problematic the unequivocal promotion of youth of color organizing as a progressive social justice movement, because the organizing is mobilized through the young people's participation in non-profit organizations and community programs that are traditionally tied to the project of managing and supervising "at-risk" youth in safe, productive spaces. Instead, youth of color organizing is more closely aligned to a discourse and mode of affirmative governmentality that promotes the participation of poor, marginalized youth in nonprofits in the exercise of personal empowerment and the building human development skills, not in the posing of challenges to state power. These programs serve as a space to train young people to mobilize collectively, but they are not separated from the joint management of young people by the state and civil society. Yet in their efforts to inform the community about the injustices of deportation at block parties, press conferences, youth conferences, rallies, and marches, AYPAL youth revealed the contradictions of neoliberal discourses and practices, while expressing an alternative vision of democracy and politics. They embodied political action as a process in the making that is arrayed against conventional notions of administrative and institutional democracy. More important, their activism demonstrates that the neoliberal state and its hegemonic projects are never complete or totalizing.

CONCLUSION

Jason, Marie, Pham, Rona, Sam, Vince, and I sat around a conference table looking out onto a bustling Telegraph Avenue in North Oakland. It was early on a Friday morning in April 2004, a month before the two-year campaign against deportation was to come to an end, and AYPAL's staff had gathered for a special meeting to discuss the status of the campaign. There was a sense of urgency: after the second press conference, with the congresswoman still showing no inclination to draft legislation to repeal the Illegal Immigration Reform and Immigrant Responsibility Act (IIRIRA), the staff feared they had a very real chance of losing their fight. Their major concern, however, was not failing to repeal the act—a goal that everyone in the room knew was out of reach—but the impact of that failure on the organization's young members. The meeting forced the staff to step back from the details of the anti-deportation campaign to discuss more generally, and at length, what they believed to be the purpose of youth organizing. Actualizing campaign demands was just part of the whole that made up AYPAL program activities after all. Marie started off the conversation: "We need to realize that we had other demands along the way in this campaign, which we knew was going to be hard. But we had other goals like raising youth political consciousness and awareness. . . . If we're going to look at this campaign only as whether we succeed in repealing the IIRIRA, then it's going to be a loss. But we said that during the process we wanted to achieve other goals of building a broader base and allies and youth learning that the system needs to change, as opposed to the fact that all we need to do is express our voices and make demands. Part of this is building youth consciousness and exposing the system." This was evident in the correlations young people were making through their work with AYPAL. Rona explained: "Youth are making connections in schools. For example, one of our youth was talking about how one of her teachers was saying that the US is the most democratic country, but she challenged that by bringing up deportation." Rona and Pham agreed that in training young people in community organizing skills, as in their work in the deportation campaign, they were building leaders in the youth organizing movement. Sam added that in addition to training youth as activists, they were building positive youth development skills. Jason felt that the group excelled in recruiting young people to become leaders and activists "because most youth organizing groups attract youth who are already part of the movement, but AYPAL doesn't. We take all the youth, even those who are not political." Marie responded: "Some youth understand the political structure, but not everyone is there yet." Vince went a step further: "It is hard to gauge. Now we can say yes, but after AYPAL? Not sure, maybe in college they will be fighting for the cause?" He went on: "What is the overall long-term goal for our youth? Beyond the campaign?"

I have repeated Vince's questions and the conversation among AYPAL staff members at this meeting here because they bring me back to a central concern of this book: the role of nonprofit organizations in promoting youth organizing and building a social justice movement. Certainly, the political aims of youth of color organizing are aligned with grassroots movements for racial and economic justice found in immigrant, working-class, and racialized communities. But youth of color organizing, as I realized after I left the field, is also tied to a particular institutional history of improving "at-risk" youth of color at the site of the nonprofit organization. In order to examine the project of youth organizing, I widened my focus from AYPAL to investigate the broader field of youth organizing and asked when, how, and why youth organizing came to represent an effective strategy of affirming youth of color as community leaders and political actors. Specifically, I described the formation in 2000 of the Funders' Collaborative on Youth Organizing (FCYO), an assemblage of funders and practitioners promoting youth organizing, in order to answer some of these questions. Since its inception, FCYO has documented the changes and issues most relevant to the field of youth organizing by conducting periodic surveys, focus groups, and interviews of members of youth organizing groups across the country. The topics raised by FCYO's reports are similar to the concerns of the AYPAL staff—not surprisingly, since the staff has participated in FCYO's studies over the years. Yet AYPAL is a different organization today than it was in the early 2000s, when I was a volunteer staff member there, and the field of youth organizing has also been refined. FCYO has thoughtfully reflected, assessed, and led the field of youth organizing in this growth. I have elaborated on some of its reports in previous chapters and add to them here, as I believe the work achieved by FCYO was essential in shaping, and continues to influence, youth of color organizing in concrete and significant ways.

Take, for example, the Regenerations: Leadership Pipeline—FCYO's latest grant initiative, launched in 2010—which tackles the most pressing concerns in the field of youth organizing: organizational funding, the youth development and youth organizing divide, and the long-term goals and transition of youth leaders.[1] To address youth organizers' concerns about the financial sustainability of nonprofit organizations, FCYO generated specific recommendations for improvement. I earlier broached the precarious position of youth organizing nonprofits that relied overwhelmingly for their survival on private foundations' resources, and how these dollars are often directed at specific topic or project grants rather than allocated as unspecified funds. To remedy this problem, FCYO now advocates for general organizational capacity grants and operating support for youth organizing nonprofits: "Capacity building grants help organizing groups to maintain and grow their work, effectively engaging young people and community members in advancing their campaigns."[2] This is a significant step toward stability for nonprofits supporting youth of color organizing. But foundations continue to drive the evaluations of viable topics and to control funds allocated for youth organizing. For instance, in June 2011, FCYO announced a funding initiative to address childhood obesity, spearheaded by a sizable grant from the Robert Wood Johnson Foundation, which funds research and programs on adolescent health issues. Despite FCYO's recommendations for general operating funds, the field of youth organizing continues to be influenced by foundations' aims and goals.

Moreover, I have shown the pressures faced by youth organizing nonprofits in producing for funders specific outcomes related to individual youth development skills rather than those concerned with the more intangible results of youth activism. I investigated how the change in the field of youth services from a "kid-fixing" model to one of "positive youth development" opened the door for a handful of private foundations to rally behind youth organizing as a viable community program and support its aims of social justice. I analyzed the significance of this paradigmatic shift, as well as its implications for youth organizing nonprofits in having to promote both positive youth development and activists' aims of producing social change. Two recent FCYO Occasional Reports, published in 2010 and 2011 as part of its Leadership Pipeline initiative, confront this matter and that of the long-term goals of youth organizing. In her FCYO report, Seema Shah attends to the youth development and youth organizing divide, demonstrating how youth development practices are integral to, not at odds with, practices of youth collective action and power analysis: "Thus, while youth organizing groups possess many elements of youth development and support the growth of young people in ways similar to youth development programs, youth organizing enhances youth development in its approach by working with young people to help them gain the knowledge and skills to understand social and structural inequities and engage in action that results in social change."[3] Shah's report signals the growing awareness by funders and other supporters of youth organizing that collective action and political practices are integral skills of youth development. In addition, it fortifies the direct intervention by youth activist practitioners, such as that made many years earlier at the FCYO meeting I attended, in which they underscored the social, not just the individual, impacts of young people's actions. It is a testament to youth organizing nonprofits that they have resisted forces to privatize citizenship practices and politics as gains of individual skills (including self-confidence, leadership, and the ability to resist drugs) and self-empowerment.

Additionally, Shawn Ginwright's 2010 FCYO report tackles the long-term goal of youth organizing. He asks: "How then do we build sustainable social justice opportunities for young people? What are the most promising strategies to build leadership capacity for the broader social justice movement? In what ways can we transition young people from high school to ongoing skill development and knowledge related to social justice efforts?"[4] To answer these questions, he delineates the three-stage leadership pipeline model espoused by FCYO, which it developed based on its 2010 field scan. He underscores the need for educational, employment, and social networks to support continued leadership opportunities and social justice–related activities for youth after high school. One of the most significant aspects of the model is that "the transition phase makes progressive movement building an explicit, rather than, implicit outcome of the pipeline."[5] As part of the Leadership Pipeline, these two reports demonstrate new energies focused on and resources available for the field of youth organizing. Crucially, they identify the immediate mechanisms within and larger linkages to societal supports outside youth nonprofit organizations to create and sustain youth of color activism over time. These reports pay serious attention to the difficulties facing youth organizing and efforts to address them.

There remains, however, an uncritical promotion of low-income youth of color to become agents of positive transformation and faith in their ability to create social change through youth organizing. For example, FCYO unequivocally states: "We truly believe that the participation and leadership of young people, particularly young people of color, are critical in achieving social justice."[6] The organization adds: "FCYO believes that youth organizing has the potential" to "challenge serious problems facing communities nationwide, especially low-income and of color communities, and work to ensure that systems and policies are accountable, equitable and fair to the communities they serve," and to "confront racism and discrimination, and its role in creating and perpetuating social inequities that disproportionately impact people of color."[7]

Notwithstanding this potential of youth of color and youth organizing, I have argued for a critical examination of the ties of youth of color organizing to nonprofit structures, the state's history of depoliticizing activism, and the powers of affirmative governmentality that are embedded in the project of youth of color organizing. I have squarely situated youth of color nonprofits and civil society as operating within, not outside of, state regulation and political economy. Nonprofit organizations must be understood in the context of the transformation from a welfare state to a neoliberal state, the increasing dependence of the state on civil society to contract its social services, and their complementary relationship to capital. Youth organizing nonprofits, as opposed to other so-called kid-fixing youth programs, were supported by and continue to depend on a select group of philanthropic foundations, entities that also maintain ties to state powers and policies. Youth organizing programs are closely tethered to the interests and investments of private foundations and state actors, which increasingly institutionalize social justice–oriented nonprofit organizations as state-regulated entities, thus posing challenges to the youth organizing movement.

As a result of my interactions with the young people of AYPAL and my participation in the youth organizing movement, I can certainly attest to the power of youth of color organizing. My point here, and in this book, is not to condemn youth organizing or its advocates. Nor is it to argue against youth organizing as an effective strategy for individual transformation or as a means of constructively engaging marginalized young people as political and social actors. Nor do I want to engage in evaluating the activism of these young people according to some idealized manifestation of social change. Rather, my intent has been to interrogate the relations of power and conditions of possibility that both enable and limit young people as political actors and democratic subjects, and I have done so through a theoretical and political critique of the assumptions, rhetorics, and practices embedded in youth of color organizing and its capacity as a progressive social justice movement. The promotion of youth of color as potentially transformative agents of individual, community, and social change through their voluntary participation overlooks an examination of not only underlying logics of the nonprofit sector but also liberal logics of empowerment. Youth activism, I argue, is implicated in an affirmative governmentality, which posits poor youth of color as potentially worthy subjects of improvement through their participation in community programs aimed at helping them to become better citizen-subjects. The productive mobilization and effects of empowerment to promote, transform, and improve are not neutral; instead, they reflect relationships of power. Youth activism is affirmed in nonprofit organizations that employ youth organizing as a positive strategy to guide youth of color so that they can become active political subjects who embrace neoliberal principles of self-responsibility and community governance.

Moreover, this mode of governance directed at empowering youth of color is not separate from the relations of power to criminalize them. Since the Progressive Era, community youth programs have been seen as a way to prevent young people from engaging in delinquency and sexual immorality. The overlapping emergence of the juvenile court system and afterschool community programs spearheaded by the efforts of philanthropists and social reformers in the early twentieth century were successful in instituting young people as a special category in need of care and regulation. Now, in the early twenty-first century, nonprofit organizations that promote youth organizing are charged with improving the life chances of "at-risk" youth of color. These nonprofits, and civil society writ large, are intricately enmeshed in the neoliberal state and its art of governance and exercise of capitalism. Youth of color organizing, and the nonprofit organizations that support it, is the latest iteration in a long tradition of social programs predicated on turning poor, marginalized youth to become better democratic subjects.

To explicate youth of color organizing as enmeshed in an affirmative governmentality, moreover, is not to argue against that organizing or against political activism. It is to seriously recognize how such projects are embedded in multiple axes of power. It is also to give equal weight to the practices that challenge them. Thus I have turned to ethnographic accounts of AYPAL members to contend that young people are not merely subjects of governance. My examination of their political practices recognized politics as collective and oppositional, but also as situated in affirmative modes of governmentality and relationships of power. Along with their partners in the multiracial coalition to stop the Super Jail, AYPAL youth openly challenged state process to target and criminalize them as "at-risk" youth. They claimed "youth of color" as a political identity, an identity that directly opposed the representation of them as "super-predators." Yet familiar strategies of racial identification and categories of politics, particularly among communities of color, are also regulated in neoliberal modes of racial incorporation and inclusion into administrative norms. The involvement of AYPAL's members in the fight against the expansion of juvenile hall, along with the lack of recognition of them as youth of color, made clear the limits of a youth of color identity politics and the need to seriously contend with the institutionalization of race as a way of managing minority groups. Activism must respond creatively to the depoliticization of race as a category of political struggle. Since the civil rights era, the neutralization of activism has been facilitated in part through the moderate redistribution of state resources to minority-based direct-services organizations, the subsequent professionalization of the nonprofit sector, and the rise of multiculturalism.

This requires an ever-pressing need among activists to resist creatively and boldly. This entails making "unlikely alliances," as Andrea Smith contends. Her thoughtful analysis of coalitional politics among evangelicals of the Christian Right and American Indian activists challenge us to rethink established routes of political organizing.[8] Moreover, as Dean Spade's work on critical transgender organizing illuminates, addressing challenges posed by poverty, criminalization, and immigration enforcement must move beyond demands for law reform and attend to the systemic norms and administrative obstacles that hinder the life chances of the most vulnerable.[9]

His example of organizing among trans rights and immigrant rights groups against the consequences of New York State's implementation of the REAL ID Act, spurred by intensified surveillance after September 11, provides an example of contemporary cross-alliance organizing.

In their efforts against deportation, AYPAL youth faced the limits of "the power of the youth" and political action in a representative democracy, underscoring the contradictory relationships of power embedded in promoting youth as engaged citizens. Their involvement in activities that constituted the core of democratic citizenship fulfilled the calls to young people to be political actors; however, their political practice was not recognized within state-sanctioned frameworks. But in this process of advocating against refugee deportation, they highlighted US policies and state modes of regulation and punishment that devalue some lives but not others. Considering that notions of good citizenship and political activity are overwhelmingly defined as individual and private acts—of volunteerism or charitable giving, for example—the public and collective action of these young people leads us to rethink the discourses and practices that constitute the political. Perhaps what is more useful than an indiscriminate promotion of youth of color as political actors is to understand the relationships of power that govern and resist their activism. Barbara Cruikshank argues that we must not separate "subjectivity from subjection in order to imagine political resistance."[10] The young people of AYPAL have not been passive receivers of management and empowerment but active participants in challenging the ruthless infringements of neoliberal powers and the atomizing logics of its governmentality.

Although I have been critical of the deployment of civil society in enabling youth empowerment and activism, I have also recognized the significance of that deployment in the mobilization of young people's oppositional political practices. Practices to resist and alter hegemonic ideas while formulating, circulating, and embodying oppositional beliefs, as evidenced by members of AYPAL and other activists, certainly resonate with Antonio Gramsci's description of "organic intellectuals."[11] In my work, these young "organic intellectuals" were central to the project of social contestation and were fostered in nonprofit organizations. This underscores the terrain of civil society as constitutive of state power and also as a possibility for political confrontation. Michel Foucault's observation of the reconfiguration of civil society as a "concept of governmental technology" informs an unmasking of nonprofit organizations as sites of neoliberal governance, as does Gramsci's expansion on state power as "political society + civil society."[12]

However, Gramsci's discussion of the changing relationship between the state and civil society and the accompanying relational forces of hegemony encourages us to devise different tactics and sites for political struggle. Stuart Hall elaborates on what he describes as Gramsci's "electrifying" conception of politics: "These emphases bring a range of new institutions and arenas of struggle into the traditional conceptualizations of the state and politics. It constitutes them as specific and strategic centres of struggle. The effect is to multiply and proliferate the various fronts of politics, and to differentiate different kinds of social antagonisms."[13] Youth of color organizing is tied to the neoliberal state's art of governance and to the logic of capitalism, which certainly restrains it as an independent social justice movement. However, those ties also allow for the practice of oppositional politics. It is necessary for us to recognize that this oppositional politics is squarely situated both in and against these relationships of power in our challenge to the duplicitous forms of domination and affirmation.

Recent scholarly and activist work has called attention to the limits of nonprofit and nongovernmental organizations and their mobilization for social change that is organized in an alleged third sector of civil society outside of the state governance or its capitalist logics.[14] Problematizing this relationship however is not meant to disregard the real movement work that some nonprofit and nongovernmental organizations are engaged in but to flag the complex relationships of power that mediate these connections.[15] Activists today are crafting responses to the consolidation of the nonprofit-industrial complex. In the summer of 2010, I attended a workshop titled Organizing beyond the Nonprofit at the second United States Social Forum (USSF), held in Detroit. I found the topic somewhat ironic for the forum, considering that over a thousand nonprofit organizations were represented there. An offshoot of the global World Social Forum, the USSF is described as an assembly and also a political process to mobilize civil society to challenge neoliberalism, imperialism, and global economic capitalism. Both the global and the national forums hold new promise for organizing, generating new energy for movements for social justice in the United States and transnationally. But we must acknowledge the fact that the USSF is not an unfettered vehicle to enable political organizing that is separate from or necessarily in opposition to the state.[16] The Organizing beyond the Nonprofit workshop, the only one I found that spoke to alternative models to nonprofit organizing, resonated among the seventy people present, who nearly filled the room. The workshop leaders and organizers called for volunteer labor, community fund-raisers and donations, and more distributive participation and democratic leadership.[17] I found refreshing the thoughtful dialogue among those in the room, which included recognition of the limits of nonprofits as well as our dependence on and links to them. To paraphrase one of the workshop organizers, nonprofit organizing is not necessarily bad, but we need to realize that it is not the only possible mode of organizing. Her comment underscores both the institutionalization of social justice organizing and our potential to confront this. Such an analysis directs us to interrogate the means by which political activism is undertaken in our struggle against the encroachment of neoliberalism. To return to this book's title, it may be that what we need are uncivil subjects, willing to inhabit bad citizenship in order to critique the supposed good faith of the state as a matter of governing ourselves. Therefore, this book's theoretical and political provocations lie in its refusal to cede to neoliberalism the categories through which we care.

NOTES

Introduction

1. In this book I use "Asian and Pacific Islander" when referring to ethnographic accounts of AYPAL, as this is how the members of the collaborative referred to the diverse racial groups represented. I use "Asian American" when I refer to the scholarship and field of Asian American studies. This usage recognizes the social constructions of racial categories and identifications as well as the competing and shifting meanings of race (see Omi and Winant, *Racial Formation*). For a discussion of shifting racial categories of Pacific Islanders, see also Diaz, "To 'P' or Not to 'P'"; Kauanui, "Asian American Studies and the 'Pacific Question'"; Toribo, "The Problematics of History."

2. Weiss, *Youth Rising*, 10.

3. A national survey of youth organizing groups found that 80 percent of these organizations had young people who came from low-income households, and white youth represented only 11 percent of young people in the groups surveyed (ibid., 72–73).

4. Californians for Justice, *Still Separate, Still Unequal*.

5. Pintado-Vertner, *The West Coast Story*.

6. Kwon, "Moving from Complaints to Action."

7. D. Edwards, Johnson, and McGillicuddy, *An Emerging Model for Working with Youth*.

8. HoSang, *Traditions and Innovations Youth Organizing in the Southwest*.

9. For an account of this organizing in California and beyond, see Brodkin, *Making Democracy Matter*; H. Gordon, *We Fight to Win*; HoSang, *Traditions and Innovations* and *Youth and Community Organizing in the Southwest*; Ishihara, *Urban Transformations*; Pintado-Vertner, *The West Coast Story*; Tait, *Poor Workers' Unions*.

10. The term "super-predator" comes from John DiIulio's article "The Coming of the Super-Predators," *Weekly Standard*, November 27, 1995, 23.

11. Most of the literature on student activism focuses on college students, whose activism holds certain privileges and is often romanticized as a passing period of rebellion. See Altbach, "Perspectives on Student Political Activism" and "Students and Politics"; Levitt, *Children of Privilege*.

12. Elizabeth Martinez, "The New Youth Movement in California," *ZMagazine*, March 2000, http://www.zcommunications.org/the-new-youth-movement-in-california-by-elizabeth-martinez, accessed August 30, 2002.

13. Foucault, *The Birth of Biopolitics*.

14. W. Brown, "Neoliberalism and the End of Liberal Democracy" and *States of Injury*; Cruikshank, *The Will to Empower*; Grewal, *Transnational America*; Joseph, *Against the Romance of Community*; Nguyen, *The Gift of Freedom*.

15. Comaroff and Comaroff, "Millennial Capitalism," 307.

16. Hartney and Silva, *And Justice for Some*.

17. Coughlin, "Prison Walls Are Crumbling," 197; Feld, "Girls in the Juvenile Justice System," 228.

18. Chesney-Lind and Shelden, *Girls, Delinquency, and Juvenile Justice*, 137.

19. Mitchell, "Pre-Black Futures."

20. Ibid., 249.

21. Cacho, *Social Death* and "'You Just Don't Know How Much He Meant.'" Also see Patton, "Refiguring Social Space."

22. Halpern, "A Different Kind of Child Development Institution," 186.

23. Foucault, *The Birth of Biopolitics*, 296. Foucault argues that the government-ability of an entrepreneurial democratic subject relies on civil society as an imagined space of sovereignty, which functions to manage the growth of this economic actor.

24. Foucault, "Governmentality." Also see Colin Gordon, "Governmental Rationality," 2.

25. Foucault, *The Birth of Biopolitics*, 44.

26. Wendy Brown expands on this point: "This mode of governmentality (techniques of governing that exceed express state action and orchestrate the subject's conduct toward him or herself) convenes a 'free' subject who rationally deliberates about alternative courses of action, makes choices, and bears responsibility for the consequences of these choices" ("Neoliberalism and the End of Liberal Democracy," 43).

27. Foucault, *The Birth of Biopolitics*, 116.

28. Drawing directly on Foucault's lectures, Wendy Brown writes: "Neo-liberalism is not simply a set of economic policies; it is not only about facilitating free trade, maximizing corporate profits, and challenging welfarism. Rather, neo-liberalism carries a social analysis which, when deployed as a form of governmentality, reaches from the soul of the citizen-subject to education policy to practices of empire. Neo-liberal rationality, while foregrounding the market, is not only or even primarily focused on the economy; rather it involves *extending and disseminating market values to all institutions and social action*, even as the market itself remains a distinctive player" ("Neoliberalism and the End of Liberal Democracy," 39–40). Also see Duggan, *The Twilight of Equality*; Harvey, *A Brief History of Neoliberalism*.

29. W. Brown, "Neoliberalism and the End of Liberal Democracy"; Cruikshank, *The Will to Empower*; Foucault, *The Birth of Biopolitics*; Rose, "The Death of the Social?" and *Governing the Soul*.

30. "About FCYO," Funders' Collaborative for Youth Organizing website, http://www.fcyo.org/aboutfcyo, accessed September 6, 2012.

31. D. Edwards, Johnson, and McGillicuddy, *An Emerging Model for Working with Youth*, 7.

32. Quoted in Shah, *Building Transformative Youth Leadership*, 34–35.

33. Cruikshank, *The Will to Empower*, 86.

34. Voters in San Francisco passed a measure to set aside 2.5 percent of the city's funds for after-school programs in 1991. The measure was mainly influenced by the work of Coleman Advocates, a nonprofit advocacy and service organization serving San Francisco's youth and families, and it was supported by a handful of private foundations, including the Evelyn and Walter Haas Jr. Fund (Eldredge, Piha, and Levin, "Building the San Francisco Beacons"; Yee, "Developing the Field of Youth Organizing and Advocacy").

35. For this shift, see Pittman et al., *Preventing Problems*, 6.

36. Rose, "The Death of the Social?," 333 and 332.

37. Weiss, *Youth Rising*, 118. See also Tang and Goldberg, *The Funders' Collaborative on Youth Organizing's Roots Initiative Toolkit*; Torres-Fleming, Valdes, and Pillai, *2010 Youth Organizing Field Scan*.

38. Cruikshank adds that the innovations of the Great Society reformers to empower the poor, and the New Left's and civil rights movement's emphases on self-government and community power, failed to solve poverty and racial inequalities but succeeded "in developing a strategy of empowerment as a solution to the problems of poverty" (*The Will to Empower*, 69).

39. Harvey, *A Brief History of Neoliberalism*, 78.

40. Gramsci, *Selections from the Prison Notebooks*, 263.

41. S. Hall, "Gramsci's Relevance for the Study of Race and Ethnicity," 18.

42. Ibid.

43. Boris, "Introduction."

44. R. Ferguson, "Administering Sexuality"; Mohanty, "On Race and Voice."

45. Fraser, *Justice Interruptus*.

46. INCITE!, *The Revolution Will Not Be Funded*.

47. Rodriguez, "The Political Logic of the Non-Profit Industrial Complex," 21–22.

48. Abramson, Salamon, and Steuerle, "Federal Spending and Tax Policies"; M. Edwards and Hulme, *Non-Governmental Organisations*; INCITE!, *The Revolution Will Not Be Funded*; Gilmore, "In the Shadow of the Shadow State"; A. Smith, "Introduction"; S. Smith and Lipsky, *Nonprofits for Hire*.

49. Gilmore, "In the Shadow of the Shadow State," 45; Michael Shuman, "Why Do Progressive Foundations Give Too Little to Too Many?," *Nation*, January 12, 1998, http://www.tni.org/archives/act/2112, accessed November 8, 2008.

50. W. Brown, "Injury, Identity, Politics"; Gordon and Newfield, "Multiculturalism's Unfinished Business"; Melamed, "The Spirit of Neoliberalism."

51. S. Smith and Lipsky, *Nonprofits for Hire*.

52. Alvarez, "Advocating Feminism"; Arnove, *Philanthropy and Cultural Imperialism*; Cruikshank, *The Will to Empower*; Dolhinow, *A Jumble of Needs*; Grewal, *Transnational America*; INCITE!, *The Revolution Will Not Be Funded*; Joseph, *Against the Romance of Community*; Karim, *Microfinance and Its Discontents*; Lashaw, "The Presence of Hope in a Movement for Equitable Schooling"; Li, *The Will to Improve*; Mindry, "Nongovernmental Organizations, 'Grassroots,' and the Politics of Virtue";

O'Neill, *The Third America*; Rudrappa, *Ethnic Routes to Becoming American.* In this manner, my project deviates from studies of social movements and their particular attention to the role of organizations, resources, and interests as mechanisms for mobilizing political actions (Ganz, "Resources and Resourcefulness"; McAdam, *Political Process and the Development of Black Insurgency*; Morris, *Origins of the Civil Rights Movement*).

53. Tang and Goldberg, *The Funders' Collaborative on Youth Organizing's Roots Initiative Toolkit*, 13.

54. S. Hall, "Gramsci's Relevance for the Study of Race and Ethnicity."

55. Maira, *Missing*.

56. Gordon, *We Fight to Win*, 8.

57. On formal modes of youth politics, see S. Bennett, "Why Young Americans Hate Politics"; Jennings and Niemi, *The Political Character of Adolescence*; Mann, "What the Survey of American College Freshmen Tells Us about Their Interest in Politics and Political Science."

58. Flanagan, "Volunteerism, Leadership, Political Socialization, and Civic Engagement"; Flanagan and Faison, "Youth Civic Development"; Kirshner, "Power in Numbers"; Levine and Youniss, *Youth Civic Engagement*; Watts and Flanagan, "Pushing the Envelope on Youth Civic Engagement"; Watts and Guessous, "Sociopolitical Development"; Youniss et al., "Youth Civic Engagement in the Twenty-First Century."

59. Cammarota and Fine, *Revolutionizing Education*; Delgado and Staples, *Youth-Led Community Organizing*; D. Edwards, Johnson, and McGillicuddy, *An Emerging Model for Working with Youth*; Ginwright, *Youth Organizing*; Ginwright and James, "From Assets to Agents of Change"; Ginwright, Noguera, and Cammarota, *Beyond Resistance!*; HoSang, *Youth and Community Organizing*; Pintado-Vertner, *The West Coast Story*; Shah, *Building Transformative Youth Leadership*.

60. D. Edwards, Johnson, and McGillicuddy, *An Emerging Model for Working with Youth*; Eccles and Appleton-Gootman, *Community Programs to Promote Youth Development*; Ginwright, *Youth Organizing*; Irby, Ferber, and Pittman, *Youth Action*; Jarrett, Sullivan, and Wilkens, "Developing Social Capital through Participation in Organized Youth Programs"; Kwon, "Moving from Complaints to Action"; R. Larson and Hansen, "The Development of Strategic Thinking"; Larson et al., "Organized Youth Activities as Contexts for Positive Development"; McLaughlin, Irby, and Langman, *Urban Sanctuaries*; Pittman and Wright, *Bridging the Gap*.

61. Volunteerism first appeared in the colonial era and expanded during the Progressive Era, the two world wars, and the 1960s civil rights and peace movements. Thereafter it declined, especially among college students in the 1980s. Programs to promote youth service included Youth Service America, Campus Outreach Opportunity League, and the AmeriCorps programs (Ellis and Noyes, *By the People*; Hodgkinson, "Individual Giving and Volunteering").

62. Abelmann, *The Intimate University*; Espiritu, *Home Bound*; Kibria, *Becoming Asian American*; Kwon, "Autoexoticizing"; J. Lee and Zhou, *Asian American Youth*; S. Lee, *Unraveling the "Model Minority" Stereotype* and *Up against Whiteness*; Maira, *Desis in the House* and *Missing*; Min, *The Second Generation*; Min and Park,

"Second Generation Asian Americans' Ethnic Identity"; Pyke and Dang, "'Fob' and 'Whitewashed'"; Shankar, *Desi Land*; N. Sharma, *Hip Hop Desis*.

63. Works by Lee (*Unraveling the "Model Minority" Stereotype* and *Up against Whiteness*), Maira (*Missing*), and Shankar (*Desi Land*) also focus on high school students of diverse economic backgrounds.

64. This is not to dismiss the debates within Asian American studies about the relationship of Pacific Islanders and Asian American studies, nor to conflate these groups (see Diaz, "To 'P' or Not to 'P'?"; Kauanui, "Asian American Studies and the 'Pacific Question'"). Rather, it is to simply note the dominant focus of East Asian groups within Asian American studies. A recent special issue of *positions* critically intervenes against this emphasis (Ngô, Nguyen, and Lam, "Southeast Asian American Studies").

65. Youth subcultural studies offered me a starting point to examine youth resistance by attending to the vivid and various cultural and oppositional practices of young people along the axes of class, race, gender, and nation. See Clarke et al., "Subcultures, Cultures, and Class"; Hebdige, *Subculture*; Ross and Rose, *Microphone Fiends*.

66. As such, this is not a detailed ethnographic account of young people's political development or of the microprocesses of young people's negotiations with their peers, adults, and surrounding institutions. I have chronicled elsewhere how AYPAL offered young people structured opportunities for collective action in supportive political community spaces (Kwon, "Moving from Complaints to Action").

67. Geertz, *The Interpretation of Cultures*.

68. The Pacific Islander group parted from the Oakland Asian Cultural Center to form its own organization, the Pacific Islander Kie Association, in 2003. Each of these organizations organized the different ethnic backgrounds of the young people: Asian Community Mental Health Services for Cambodian, Filipinos for Affirmative Action for Filipino/a, the Korean Community Center of the East Bay for Korean, the Lao Iu Mien Cultural Association for Laotian and Mien, the Oakland Asian Student Educational Services for Chinese and Vietnamese, and the Pacific Islander Kie Association for Samoan and Tongan.

69. All the names of AYPAL participants in this book are pseudonyms.

70. Chung, *Legacies of Struggle*; Das Gupta, *Unruly Immigrants*; Habal, *San Francisco's International Hotel*; Rudrappa, *Ethnic Routes to Becoming American*; Võ, *Mobilizing an Asian American Community*.

71. Ong and Liu, "U.S. Immigration Policies and Asia Migration," 45.

72. Ma, *Hometown Chinatown*, 109.

73. The statistics are from US Bureau of the Census, "Summary File 2 (SF2) 100-Percent Data." Although ethnic subgroups among Laotians are not reported in the census, the largest portion of Laotians in Oakland are Mien. It was estimated that of the approximately 30,000 Mien refugees living in the United States, 5,000 resided in Oakland (Neela Banerjee, "Lao Iu Mien Culture Center Breaks Ground," *Asian Week*, November 2, 2000, http://www.asianweek.com/2000_10_26/home.html, accessed December 17, 2001).

74. During my time with AYPAL, it paid a small stipend to its youth interns, as

did many other youth organizing groups. In doing so, the group recognized the importance of young people's employment needs—whether to supplement their family income or to have spending money. Many of the AYPAL youth admitted that the stipend was not nearly equal to what they would get from working at McDonald's or Starbucks. Some of them did supplement their stipend by working on weekends at movie theaters or businesses such as Walgreens.

75. Gilmore, *Golden Gulag*; Hale, *Engaging Contradictions, Theory, Politics, and Methods of Activist Scholarship*; Juris, "Social Forums and Their Margins"; Sanford and Ajani, *Engaged Observer*.

1. Civilizing Youth against Delinquency

1. Platt, *The Child Savers*, 10. Although special programs to deal with juvenile delinquency existed before the late nineteenth century, it was not until the establishment of the first juvenile court in Illinois that these reforms were rationalized into a coherent system of juvenile justice (ibid., xviii). Other states followed suit, with thirty-two establishing juvenile courts by 1910; all but two states had done so by 1925 (Office of Juvenile Justice and Delinquency Prevention, *Juvenile Justice*, 2).

2. Platt, "The Triumph of Benevolence," 367.

3. Platt, *The Child Savers*, xx.

4. Kennedy, "Eugenics, 'Degenerate Girls,' and Social Workers during the Progressive Era"; Nathanson, *Dangerous Passage*; Platt, "The Triumph of Benevolence." For the demographic constitution of European immigrants during this time, see Roediger, *Working toward Whiteness*, 11.

5. Immigrants, the poor, members of racial minority groups, the working class, and youth were not the only targets of intervention: "During the Progressive Era, many people were categorized as degeneratively unfit, including sexually active, unmarried women and adolescent girls (the latter commonly defined as delinquent), as well as paupers, criminals, gays and lesbians, epileptics, alcoholics, the mentally ill, and the mentally retarded" (Kennedy, "Eugenics, 'Degenerate Girls,' and Social Workers during the Progressive Era," 24).

6. G. Hall, *Adolescence*. Hall was at the forefront of establishing adolescence as a universal category of knowledge and as a physical and emotional phase of human development through the discipline of psychology. He was the first recipient of a doctorate in psychology from Harvard University, in 1887. He founded and edited the *American Journal of Psychology* and was part of the planning team that in 1892 created the American Psychological Association, whose first president he was.

7. Scholars have critiqued Hall's ahistorical and universal representation of adolescence by deconstructing "youth" as a distinct biological, cultural, and generational age group. See Cote and Allahar, *Generation on Hold*; Griffin, *Representations of Youth*; Lesko, "Denaturalizing Adolescence."

8. Cruikshank, *The Will to Empower*, 40.

9. Halpern, "A Different Kind of Child Development Institution," 181.

10. Addams, *The Spirit of Youth and the City Streets*, 102–3.

11. Bryan and Davis, "Beginnings," 6–7.

12. Ibid., 5.

13. Halpern, *Making Play Work*, 21.

14. K. Larson, "The Saturday Evening Girls," 196.

15. Platt, *The Child Savers*, 121. See also Chesney-Lind and Shelden, *Girls, Delinquency, and Juvenile Justice*; Zimring, *American Juvenile Justice*. By the early nineteenth century, the United States had established clear rules of criminal responsibility, which leaned toward the protection and benefit of the child. For instance, children under seven years of age were presumed incapable of committing crimes, and children between seven and fourteen were considered "destitute of criminal design" unless "guilty knowledge [was] shown" (Platt, *The Child Savers*, 198).

16. Platt, *The Child Savers*, 138.

17. Ibid., 103.

18. Platt, "The Triumph of Benevolence," 375, 378.

19. A. Davis, "Introduction," xx–xxi.

20. Platt, "The Triumph of Benevolence," 379.

21. These women included Louise deKoven Bowen, Mary Rozet Smith, Anita McCormick Blaine, Mary Wilmarth, Sara Hart, and Helen Culver—all daughters of prominent families (Bryan and Davis, "Beginnings," 7). Bowen in particular was an important and major benefactor of the Hull House; she was a member of the Chicago Woman's Club and Hull House Woman's Club, on whose behalf she funded an auditorium, "Bowen Hall," to fit 800 people when the club's membership grew. She came from an elite Chicago family of businessmen with strong ties to the city's political leaders, and she married a prominent banker (Platt, *The Child Savers*, 87).

22. For instance, "Pauline Agassiz Shaw was the daughter of the famous nineteenth-century naturalist, Louis Agassiz, and the stepdaughter of Elizabeth Cary Agassiz, founder of Radcliffe College for women, in Cambridge, Massachusetts" (K. Larson, "The Saturday Evening Girls," 203).

23. A. Davis, "Introduction"; Kennedy, "Eugenics, 'Degenerate Girls,' and Social Workers during the Progressive Era"; K. Larson, "The Saturday Evening Girls"; Nathanson, *Dangerous Passage*; Platt, *The Child Savers*.

24. Chesney-Lind and Shelden, *Girls, Delinquency, and Juvenile Justice*; Odem, *Delinquent Daughters*; Platt, *The Child Savers*.

25. Platt, *The Child Savers*, 79.

26. Halpern, "A Different Kind of Child Development Institution," 188.

27. Bryan and Davis, "Beginnings," 7.

28. K. Larson, "The Saturday Evening Girls," 204.

29. Halpern, *Making Play Work*, 27.

30. Addams, *The Spirit of the Youth and the City Streets*, 52.

31. Ibid., 27.

32. Ibid., 97.

33. Kennedy, "Eugenics, 'Degenerate Girls,' and Social Workers during the Progressive Era," 27.

34. Odem, *Delinquent Daughters*, 3.
35. Nathanson, *Dangerous Passage*, 121.
36. Ibid.
37. K. Larson, "The Saturday Evening Girls," 208.
38. Platt, *The Child Savers*, 3–4.
39. Ibid., 138.
40. Addams, *The Spirit of the Youth and the City Streets*, 55–57.
41. Nathanson, *Dangerous Passage*, 107.
42. Chesney-Lind and Shelden, *Girls, Delinquency, and Juvenile Justice*; Nathanson, *Dangerous Passage*.
43. Chesney-Lind and Shelden, *Girls, Delinquency, and Juvenile Justice*, 167.
44. Ibid., 168.
45. Nathanson, *Dangerous Passage*, 117.
46. Ibid., 132.
47. Chesney-Lind and Shelden, *Girls, Delinquency, and Juvenile Justice*, 165.
48. Ibid., 167.
49. Ibid., 202–3.
50. Platt, *The Child Savers*, 150.
51. Platt, "The Triumph of Benevolence," 367.
52. Platt, *The Child Savers*, 103.
53. Office of Juvenile Justice and Delinquency Prevention, "Juvenile Justice," 4.
54. Gilmore, *Golden Gulag*, 110.
55. Gilmore, *Golden Gulag*; Glassner, *Culture of Fear*; Males, *Scapegoat Generation*; Office of Juvenile Justice and Delinquency Prevention, "Juvenile Justice"; Zimring, *American Youth Violence*.
56. Gilmore, *Golden Gulag*, 109.
57. Collins and Kearns, "Under Curfew and under Siege?"; Nicole Davis, "Schoolground or Police State?," *ColorLines*, December 10, 1999, http://colorlines.com/archives/1999/12/schoolground_or_police_state.html, accessed December 17, 2007; Meiners, *Right to Be Hostile*.
58. Males, *Framing Youth*.
59. Feld, *Bad Kids*, 5; Office of Juvenile Justice and Delinquency Prevention, "Juvenile Justice."
60. For a more detailed account, see Feld, *Bad Kids*; Office of Juvenile Justice and Delinquency Prevention, "Juvenile Justice." A few other cases in this series are *Kent v. United States* (1966), *In re Winship* (1970), and *Breed v. Jones* (1975).
61. John DiIulio, "The Coming of the Super-Predators," *Weekly Standard*, November 27, 1995, 23. The super-predator thesis was extended when DiIulio and his colleagues blamed the growing population of what DiIulio (in ibid.) called "stone-cold predators" on the moral poverty of single-parent homes (Bennett, DiIulio, and Walters, *Body Count*).
62. Glassner, *Culture of Fear*; Males, *Scapegoat Generation* and *Framing Youth*; Meiners, *Right to Be Hostile*; Zimring, *American Youth Violence*.
63. Males, *Framing Youth*, 22.

64. Feld, "Girls in the Juvenile Justice System," 229.

65. Gilmore, *Golden Gulag*; Males, *Scapegoat Generation* and *Framing Youth*; Zimring, *American Youth Violence*.

66. Males, *Framing Youth*, 6.

67. Office of Juvenile Justice and Delinquency Prevention, "Juvenile Justice."

68. Coughlin, "Prison Walls Are Crumbling," 197.

69. Chesney-Lind and Pasko, *The Female Offender*, 3.

70. Chesney-Lind and Shelden, *Girls, Delinquency, and Juvenile Justice*, 235.

71. Feld, "Girls in the Juvenile Justice System," 263.

72. Chesney-Lind and Shelden, *Girls, Delinquency, and Juvenile Justice*, 235.

73. Luker, *Dubious Conceptions*; Nathanson, *Dangerous Passage*.

74. Nathanson, *Dangerous Passage*, 25.

75. Luker, *Dubious Conceptions*, 12.

76. Nathanson, *Dangerous Passage*, 162.

77. Muncie and Hughes, "Modes of Youth Governance," 13.

2. Youth Organizing and Nonprofitization

1. Task Force on Youth Development and Community Programs, *A Matter of Time*, 17.

2. Ibid., 9–10.

3. Lubeck and Garrett, "The Social Construction of the 'At-Risk' Child."

4. Task Force on Youth Development and Community Programs, *A Matter of Time*, 13 and 15.

5. Centers for Disease Control and Prevention, "Youth Risk Behavior Surveillance," 2.

6. Task Force on Youth Development and Community Programs, *A Matter of Time*, 10.

7. Mitchell, "Pre-Black Futures," 249.

8. O'Connor, "Community Action, Urban Reform, and the Fight against Poverty"; Regal, *Oakland's Partnership for Change*; Shiao, *Identifying Talent, Institutionalizing Diversity*; Viorst, *The Citizen Poor of the 1960's*.

9. J. M. Regal notes that the Gray Areas Program in Oakland expanded its programs in the second phase to include adults only after the Ford Foundation's officers realized the integral role of adults in supporting young people: "The concern of the Foundation at this time [first phase] was primarily focused on youth. . . . As the Foundation broadened their perspective for social intervention, they also gave greater recognition to the role of adults in the life of youth. Adults, in their supportive role to youth, became a secondary target for intervention" (*Oakland's Partnership for Change*, 3).

10. Alice O'Connor shows how the increasing focus by Gray Areas Program staff and private reforms in the War on Poverty on behavioral deficiencies and the "culture of the poor" led reformers to lose sight of the larger forces of structural economic and political marginalization ("Community Action, Urban Reform, and

the Fight against Poverty," 616). Oakland was the only site in which a local city government was the recipient of the Ford Foundation grant. For Gray Areas Programs in other areas, the foundation dispersed money to a new corporation designed to coordinate public and private agencies working with the poor (Shiao, *Identifying Talent, Institutionalizing Diversity*).

11. Regal, *Oakland's Partnership for Change*.

12. Cloward and Ohlin, *Delinquency and Opportunity*.

13. Hagan, *Introduction to Criminology*; Lanier and Henry, *Essentialist Criminology*.

14. Lanier and Henry, *Essentialist Criminology*.

15. Livingston, *Student's Guide to Landmark Congressional Laws on Social Security and Welfare*, 116.

16. Task Force on Youth Development and Community Programs, *A Matter of Time*, 11.

17. Ibid.

18. Ibid., 15.

19. Irby, Ferber, and Pittman, *Youth Action*; Pittman and Irby, *An Advocate's Guide to Youth Development*; Pittman and Wright, *Bridging the Gap*; Pittman et al., *Preventing Problems*.

20. Pittman and Wright, *Bridging the Gap*.

21. Ibid., 3.

22. Other reports on positive youth development by Pittman, Irby, and colleagues include Irby, Ferber, and Pittman, *Youth Action*; Pittman and Irby, *An Advocate's Guide to Youth Development*; Pittman and Wright, *Bridging the Gap*; Pittman et al., *Preventing Problems*.

23. Irby, Ferber, and Pittman, *Youth Action*, 11.

24. Pittman and Wright, *Bridging the Gap*, 6.

25. D. Edwards, Johnson, and McGillicuddy, *An Emerging Model for Working with Youth*.

26. For this shift to youth engagement and youth action, see Pittman et al., *Preventing Problems*, 6.

27. Irby, Ferber, and Pittman, *Youth Action*, 2.

28. Pittman et al., *Preventing Problems*, 6.

29. D. Edwards, Johnson, and McGillicuddy, *An Emerging Model for Working with Youth*, 7.

30. Yee, "Developing the Field of Youth Organizing and Advocacy," 111–12.

31. Ibid., 112–13.

32. Wallace, "Foundations Putting Money into Campaigns Led by Youths."

33. HoSang, *Youth and Community Organizing*, 17–18.

34. Ginwright, *Building a Pipeline for Justice*, 8.

35. Torres-Fleming, Valdes, and Pillai, *2010 Youth Organizing Field Scan*.

36. Sullivan, "The State of Youth Organizing," 27.

37. Ibid.

38. "Home," FCYO website, http://www.fcyo.org, accessed September 6, 2012.

39. D. Edwards, Johnson, and McGillicuddy, *An Emerging Model for Working with Youth*, 23.

40. Sullivan, "The State of Youth Organizing," 28.

41. Tang and Goldberg, *The Funders' Collaborative on Youth Organizing's Roots Initiative Toolkit*, 102.

42. Weiss, *Youth Rising*, 72–73.

43. D. Edwards, Johnson, and McGillicuddy, *An Emerging Model for Working with Youth*, 6.

44. Ibid., 9.

45. Yee, "Developing the Field of Youth Organizing and Advocacy," 123.

46. D. Edwards, Johnson, and McGillicuddy, *An Emerging Model for Working with Youth*, 7.

47. Ibid., 2–3.

48. Yee, "Developing the Field of Youth Organizing and Advocacy," 113.

49. Ibid., 114.

50. Foucault, *The Birth of Biopolitics*, 143.

51. Ibid., 145.

52. Ibid., 144.

53. Joseph, *Against the Romance of Community.*

54. Rose, "The Death of the Social?," 349.

55. Shahidullah, *Crime Policy in America*, 17.

56. Yee, "Developing the Field of Youth Organizing and Advocacy," 111.

57. Boris, "Introduction"; Galaskiewicz and Bielefeld, *Nonprofit Organizations in an Age of Uncertainty*; Joseph, *Against the Romance of Community*; A. Smith, "Introduction."

58. Joseph, *Against the Romance of Community*, 91.

59. Gilmore, "In the Shadow of the Shadow State," 45.

60. Espiritu, *Asian American Panethnicity*, 86; Piven and Cloward, *Poor People's Movements.*

61. A string of federal laws in the 1960s made racial discrimination explicitly illegal and sought to guarantee access for and expand the representation of racial minority groups in the political arena, the workplace, and social settings. The passage of the Civil Rights Act and Economic Opportunity Act in 1964 forbade racial discrimination in public places and required employers to provide equal employment opportunities to all racial groups. Executive Order 11246 further reinforced equal opportunity programs in federal employment and required government contractors to take explicit affirmative action in order to ensure against racial discrimination and increase racial diversity in the workplace.

62. Espiritu, *Asian American Panethnicity*, 86.

63. Ma, *Hometown Chinatown*, 119.

64. Ibid., 130.

65. Duggan, *The Twilight of Equality*; INCITE!, *The Revolution Will Not Be Funded*; Piven and Cloward, *Poor People's Movements.*

66. Espiritu, *Asian American Panethnicity*; Hawk, "Native Organizing before the Non-Profit Industrial Complex"; Võ, *Mobilizing an Asian American Community.*

67. Espiritu, *Asian American Panethnicity*; Võ, *Mobilizing an Asian American Community.*

68. INCITE!, *The Revolution Will Not Be Funded.*

69. W. Brown, *States of Injury.*

70. Blaustein, *The American Promise*; Gronbjerg and Salamon, "Devolution, Marketization, and the Changing Shape of Government-Nonprofit Relations"; Harder, Musselwhite, and Salamon, *Government Spending and the Nonprofit Sector in San Francisco*; Marable, *Race, Reform, and Rebellion*; O'Connor, "Community Action, Urban Reform, and the Fight against Poverty"; Peck, *Workfare States*; Pierson, *Dismantling the Welfare State?*; Piven and Cloward, *Poor People's Movements*; S. Smith and Lipsky, *Nonprofits for Hire.*

71. Piven and Cloward, *Poor People's Movements*, 354.

72. Gans, *The War against the Poor.* For instance, President Ronald Reagan's election in 1981 led to devastating cuts in job training programs such as the Comprehensive Employment and Training Act, the federal Food Stamps Program, subsidized housing projects under the Department of Housing and Urban Development, and Neighborhood Stabilization Programs earmarked for inner cities (Marable, *Race, Reform, and Rebellion*).

73. Halpern, *Making Play Work*, 72.

74. Ibid., 72–73.

75. S. Smith and Lipsky, *Nonprofits for Hire*, vii.

76. Harder, Musselwhite, and Salamon, *Government Spending and the Nonprofit Sector in San Francisco*, xv and 26.

77. Ibid.

78. S. Smith and Lipsky, *Nonprofits for Hire.*

79. Galaskiewicz and Bielefeld, *Nonprofit Organizations in an Age of Uncertainty*, vii.

80. Salamon, "The Resilient Sector."

81. Ibid., 7.

82. Joseph, *Against the Romance of Community*, 70.

83. A. Smith, "Introduction," 4.

84. Ibid., 5.

85. Ibid., 6.

86. Joseph, *Against the Romance of Community*, 91.

87. Allen, *Black Awakening in Capitalist America*; Arnove, *Philanthropy and Cultural Imperialism*; Joseph, *Against the Romance of Community*; A. Smith, "Introduction"; Proietto, "The Ford Foundation and Women's Studies in Media Higher Education."

88. Allen, *Black Awakening in Capitalist America*; O'Connor, "Community Action, Urban Reform, and the Fight against Poverty"; Shiao, *Identifying Talent, Institutionalizing Diversity*; A. Smith, "Introduction."

89. Allen, *Black Awakening in Capitalist America*, 61.

90. Shiao, *Identifying Talent, Institutionalizing Diversity*, 197.

91. Espiritu and Omi, "Who Are You Calling Asian?," 50.

92. Ibid., 50–51.

93. Kwon, "The Politics and Institutionalization of a Panethnic Identity."

94. R. Ferguson, "Administering Sexuality," 163. For an excellent critique of the

normalization of race, sex, and poverty as neutral features of state administrative systems, see Spade, *Normal Life*.

95. Shiao, *Identifying Talent, Institutionalizing Diversity*, 165.

96. Ibid.

97. Weiss, *Youth Rising*, 83.

98. Sullivan, "The State of Youth Organizing," 29.

99. Tang and Goldberg, *The Funders' Collaborative on Youth Organizing's Roots Initiative Toolkit*, 17.

100. Weiss, *Youth Rising*, 84.

101. Torres-Fleming, Valdes, and Pillai, *2010 Youth Organizing Field Scan*, 4.

102. As I mentioned in the introduction, AYPAL is a collaborative that draws young people from six ethnic nonprofit organizations in Oakland. These organizations are generally concerned with politically neutral direct services such as translation, immigrant assistance, mental health treatment, and psychological counseling. It is only in the AYPAL collaborative that the young people engage in youth organizing and community leadership activities. (This arrangement was not unusual to AYPAL; rather, it was common for youth organizing nonprofits to have parent organizations focusing on direct services.)

103. Fulbright-Anderson et al., "Structural Racism and Youth Development," 46; Michael Shuman, "Why Do Progressive Foundations Give Too Little to Too Many?," *Nation*, January 12, 1998, http://www.tni.org/archives/act/2112, accessed November 8, 2008.

104. Tang and Goldberg, *The Funders' Collaborative on Youth Organizing's Roots Initiative Toolkit*, 17.

105. Shah, *Building Transformative Youth Leadership*, 35–36.

106. Tang and Goldberg, *The Funders' Collaborative on Youth Organizing's Roots Initiative Toolkit*, 15. The tension between providing youth development and social change outcomes is echoed in many of the reports on youth organizing. In addition to Tang and Goldberg, see D. Edwards, Johnson, and McGillicuddy, *An Emerging Model for Working with Youth*; Ginwright, *Building a Pipeline for Justice*, 14–16; HoSang, *Youth and Community Organizing*, 15; Torres-Fleming, Valdes, and Pillai, *2010 Youth Organizing Field Scan*.

107. Jason reinforced this point in an interview with me: "I think that youth organizing will always have a large part of it that's direct services. Because it's youth development also. You can't separate youth development. . . . In youth organizing, youth development is intermeshed within the whole program."

108. Torres-Fleming, Valdes, and Pillai, *2010 Youth Organizing Field Scan*, 17.

109. Sullivan, "The State of Youth Organizing," 28.

110. Kwon, "Moving from Complaints to Action."

111. R. Brown, *Black Girlhood Celebration*.

3. Organizing against Criminalization

1. Donna Horowitz, "Juvenile Hall Says It Overstated Youth Violence," *Oakland Tribune*, March 9, 2001.

2. Adam Liptack, "U.S. Prison Population Dwarfs That of Other Nations," *New York Times*, April 23, 2008, http://www.nytimes.com/2008/04/23/world/americas/23iht-23prison.12253738.html?pagewanted=all, accessed May 10, 2008.

3. *Books Not Bars*, directed by Mark Landsman (New York: Witness, 2001).

4. Activists also argued that the proposed site was "too far from home" for Oakland residents, making family visitations difficult.

5. Horowitz, "Juvenile Hall Says It Overstated Youth Violence."

6. For an account of progressive hip-hop tradition in the Bay Area, see Harrison, *Hip Hop Underground*. For an account of the prominent role of hip-hop in youth organizing in Oakland, see Gordon, *We Fight to Win*; Tilton, *Dangerous or Endangered*.

7. For an account of organizing movements in Oakland, see Rhomberg, *No There There*; Self, *American Babylon*.

8. A. Ferguson, *Bad Boys*, 83.

9. Horowitz, "Juvenile Hall Says It Overstated Youth Violence."

10. Gilmore, *Golden Gulag*, 7.

11. Wordes, Krisberg, and Barry, *Facing the Future*, 1.

12. Zimring, *American Juvenile Justice*, 162.

13. Tilton, *Dangerous or Endangered*, 210.

14. Ibid., 20. Tilton provides an excellent account of the Super Jail campaign.

15. Rose, "The Death of the Social?"

16. Krisberg and Austin, *Reinventing Juvenile Justice*; Schwartz, *(In)Justice for Juveniles*; Shelden, *Detention Diversion Advocacy*.

17. EdSource, *How California Ranks: A National Perspective*, 4.

18. Meiners, *Right to Be Hostile*, 16.

19. A 1998 report from the National Center for Education Statistics indicated that the number of reported violent incidents in schools had declined or stayed about the same since 1976 (ibid., 32).

20. Advancement Project and Civil Rights Project, *Opportunities Suspended*, 7.

21. HoSang, *Youth and Community Organizing*.

22. Pulido, "Development of the 'People of Color' Identity in the Environmental Justice Movement of the Southwestern United States" and *Black, Brown, Yellow and Left*.

23. Kwon, "The Institutionalization of a Panethnic Identity."

24. Palumbo-Liu, *Asian/American*, 173.

25. Kim, "Asian Americans Are People of Color, Too . . . Aren't They?," 27. The fact that Asian Americans have very different opinions about various political issues and do not align as a group with either of the two major political parties, unlike African Americans and Latinos, also fuels this ambiguity.

26. Le et al., *Not Invisible: Asian Pacific Islander Juvenile Arrests in Alameda County*, 4.

27. Le et al., *Not Invisible: Asian Pacific Islander Juvenile Arrests in San Francisco County*, 4.

28. Le, "Delinquency among Asian/Pacific Islanders," 57.

29. Sajid Farooq, "Defending Our Youth: A Coalition of Activists Fight against

Alameda's Proposed Juvenile Detention Facility," *AsianWeek*, August 7, 2002, http://asianweek.com/2002_08_02/feature.html, accessed August 30, 2002.

30. D. Rodriguez, "Asian-American Studies in the Age of the Prison Industrial Complex."

31. A. Smith, "Heteropatriarchy and the Three Pillars of White Supremacy."

32. W. Brown, *States of Injury*; Chuh, *Imagine Otherwise*; Duggan, *The Twilight of Equality*; R. Ferguson, "Administering Sexuality"; Lowe, *Immigrant Acts*.

33. Grewal, *Transnational America*, 14.

34. A. Ong, *Buddha Is Hiding*.

35. Mori Nishida wrote in the activist Asian American newspaper *Gidra* in August 1970: "The kind of changes we are talking about when we say, 'Serve the People,' is institutional change. This means structural development of new community institutions to serve the people. Structural changes of new institutions would make change permanent" ("Serve the People," 306).

36. Aguirre and Lio, "Spaces of Mobilization"; Geron, "Serve the People"; Wei, *The Asian American Movement*.

37. This arrangement was what was most sensible for the group at the time I worked with them. The organizing structure of AYPAL is different today.

38. Gordon and Newfield, "Multiculturalism's Unfinished Business."

39. Melamed, "The Spirit of Neoliberalism," 19.

40. Omi and Winant, *Racial Formation in the United States*, 147.

41. Kwon, "The Institutionalization of a Panethnic Identity."

42. Kauanui, "Asian American Studies and the 'Pacific Question,'" 134.

4. Confronting the State

1. Number given in an e-mail correspondence with Returnee Integration Support Center staff member on July 20, 2010.

2. Momo Chang, "Life after 9/11," *Hyphen*, November 2, 2008, http://www.hyphen magazine.com/print/1679, accessed December 2, 2008.

3. The exclusionary provisions for deporting aliens for criminal activity were actually put into place earlier by the Immigration Act of 1990. However, amendments and changes in both the Anti-Terrorism and Effective Death Penalty Act and IIRIRA facilitated deportations. For information on these two laws, see Capps, Hagan, and Rodriguez, "Border Residents Manage the U.S. Immigration and Welfare Reforms"; Dow, "Designed to Punish"; Farnam, *US Immigration Laws under the Threat of Terrorism*; Freeman, "Client Politics or Populism?"; Hing, "Deporting Cambodian Refugees"; Morawetz, "Rethinking Retroactive Deportation Laws and the Due Process Clause" and "Understanding the Impact of the 1996 Deportation Laws and the Limited Scope of Proposed Reforms"; Park and Park, *Probationary Americans*; and Shuck, *Citizens, Strangers, and In-Betweens*.

4. Farnam, *US Immigration Laws under the Threat of Terrorism*.

5. Brotherton and Kretsedemas, *Keeping Out the Other*; Cole, *Enemy Aliens*; DeGenova, "Migrant 'Illegality' and Deportability in Everyday Life"; DeGenova

and Peutz, *The Deportation Regime*; Maira, "Deporting Radicals, Deporting *La Migra*"; Volpp, "The Citizen and the Terrorist."

6. Maira, *Missing*, 23.

7. For a discussion of deportation as a racialized regime of state power, see DeGenova, "Migrant 'Illegality' and Deportability in Everyday Life"; Maira, "Deporting Radicals, Deporting *La Migra*."

8. Park and Park, *Probationary Americans*, 56.

9. Joe Cochrane and Adam Piore, "A Bitter Bon Voyage," *Newsweek International*, August 5, 2002, 27; Park and Park, *Probationary Americans*, 56.

10. For an excellent account of how US imperial logic ties acts of military violence to benevolence toward refugees, see Nguyen, *The Gift of Freedom*.

11. If no formal forced removal agreements existed between a detainee's home country and the United States, the maximum time a person could be held in detention centers was nine months. Yet this rule was not always enforced. AYPAL members learned of people whose family members were moved directly from prison to detention centers for longer than nine months, with no plan of release. Moreover, detainees are often moved across the country from one facility to another; the law does not require that family members be notified of these moves. For more information, see Seng, "Cambodian Nationality Law under the Illegal Immigration Reform and Immigrant Responsibility Act."

12. American Civil Liberties Union, "ACLU Amicus Brief in Reno v. Ma," February 21, 2000, http://www.aclu.org/content/aclu-amicus-brief-reno-v-ma, accessed September 10, 2012; Dow, *American Gulag*, 273.

13. Randall Richard, "Banned for Life: Jailed at 17, Kim Ho Ma Can Never Live in America," *AsianWeek*, November 21, 2003, http://www.asianweek.com/2003/11/21/banned-for-life-jailed-at-17-kim-ho-ma-can-never-live-in-america/, accessed September 16, 2012 .

14. Taylor, "*Demore v. Kim*," 344.

15. Mansbridge, *Beyond Adversary Democracy*; Pateman, *Participation and Democratic Theory*; Walzer, *Obligations*.

16. Simanski and Sapp, *Immigration Enforcement Actions: 2011*, 1.

17. Seth Freed Wessler, "U.S. Deports 46k Parents with Citizen Kids in Just Six Months," *Color Lines*, November 3, 2011, http://colorlines.com, accessed September 16, 2012.

18. Leti Volpp usefully outlines four discourses of citizenship: citizenship as legal status, citizenship as rights, citizenship as political activity, citizenship as identity that includes practices of inclusion and exclusion ("The Citizen and the Terrorist," 156).

19. Maira, *Missing*, 248.

20. *Sentenced Home*, directed by David Grabias and Nicole Newnham (New York: Indiepix, 2006); Deborah Sontag, "In a Homeland Far from Home," *New York Times Magazine*, November 16, 2003.

21. Quoted in Sontag, "In a Homeland Far from Home," 52.

22. *Sentenced Home*.

23. Walter Leitner International Human Rights Clinic, Returnee Integration Support Center, and Deported Diaspora, *Removing Refugees*.

24. Zilberg, "Refugee Gang Youth."

25. For more information on the Khmer Rouge, see Chandler, *Voices from S-21* and *A History of Cambodia*; Hein, *From Vietnam, Laos, and Cambodia*; Hinton, *Why Did They Kill?*

26. Quoted in Sontag, "In a Homeland Far from Home."

27. Hein, *From Vietnam, Laos, and Cambodia*; Hing, "Deporting Cambodian Refugees"; Loescher and Scanlan, *Calculated Kindness*.

28. L. Gordon, "Southeast Asian Refugee Migration to the United States"; Hing, "Deporting Cambodian Refugees"; Loescher and Scanlan, *Calculated Kindness*.

29. By 1980, about 45 percent of the first wave of Southeast Asian refugees had resettled to urban cities, seeking communities of people from their former homelands (Hing, "Deporting Cambodian Refugees," 272).

30. Sontag, "In a Homeland Far from Home."

31. Ibid.

32. US Bureau of the Census, "Summary File 1 (SF1) 100-Percent Data."

33. Ung, *First They Killed My Father*.

34. Dougherty, Wilson, and Wu, "Immigration Enforcement Actions," 6.

35. For a discussion of how young Muslim youth mediated different forms of citizenship and practices that were against, complicit with, and even ambivalent about the state, see Maira, *Missing*.

36. Das Gupta, *Unruly Immigrants*, 22.

37. R. Rodriguez and Balce, "American Insecurity and Radical Filipino Community Politics," 137.

38. Naber, "So Our History Doesn't Become Your Future" and "The Rules of Forced Engagement."

39. Grewal, *Transnational America*, 22.

40. W. Brown, *States of Injury*, 5.

Conclusion

1. The initiative is described by FCYO in this way: "In 2010, in response to the deepened interest in supporting young people to develop holistically as leaders and the field of youth organizing's growth and self-articulated needs, FCYO launched its Leadership Pipeline Initiative, a multiyear strategy to address sustainability of social change efforts by cultivating the leadership of low-income youth of color, systematically and intentionally, over time" (quoted in Shah, *Building Transformative Youth Leadership*, 34).

2. Shah, *Building Transformative Youth Leadership*, 34

3. Ibid., 4.

4. Ginwright, *Building a Pipeline for Justice*, 16.

5. Ibid., 20.

6. "Home," FCYO website, http://fcyo.org/, accessed September 14, 2012.

7. "About Youth Organizing," FCYO website, http://fcyo.org/about youth organizing, accessed February 15, 2010.

8. A. Smith, *Native Americans and the Christian Right*.

9. Spade, *Normal Life*.

10. Cruikshank, *The Will to Empower*, 120.

11. Gramsci, *Selections from the Prison Notebooks of Antonio Gramsci*, 15.

12. Foucault, *The Birth of Biopolitics*, 296; Gramsci, *Selections from the Prison Notebooks of Antonio Gramsci*, 263.

13. S. Hall, "Gramsci's Relevance for the Study of Race and Ethnicity," 19–20.

14. Alvarez, "Advocating Feminism"; Bumiller, *In an Abusive State*; Dolhinow, *A Jumble of Needs*; INCITE!, *The Revolution Will Not Be Funded*; Joseph, *Against the Romance of Community*; Karim, *Microfinance and Its Discontents*; Li, *The Will to Improve*; Mindry, "Nongovernmental Organizations, 'Grassroots,' and the Politics of Virtue"; Rudrappa, *Ethnic Routes to Becoming American*; A. Sharma, *Logics of Empowerment*; Spade, *Normal Life*.

15. For a nuanced discussion of nongovernmental organizations and social movement work, see Alvarez, "Beyond Ngo-ization?"

16. Members of the National Planning Committee of the USSF came from various national and local nonprofit organizations. Although the committee made a conscious effort to prioritize grassroots fund-raising, including "passing the hat activities," registration fees, and organizational support, almost half (46 percent) of the funding for the USSF came from foundations. Michael Guerrero, a member of the committee, noted: "The USSF had fairly strict limits in terms of allowable sources. Corporations were not allowed to contribute (except through foundations), governments were only allowed to provide in-kind support" ("You Can't Spell Fundraising without F-U-N," 72).

17. These comments echo the call by scholar-activists for nonprofit and community organizations to make a break from foundations and state sources (INCITE!, *The Revolution Will Not Be Funded*). Others propose an entrepreneurial model in which nonprofits generate their own income to sustain their organizations and work (Michael Shuman and Merrian Fuller, "Profits for Justice," *Nation*, January 24, 2005, http://www.thenation.com/article/profits-justice, accessed February 5, 2010).

REFERENCES

Abelmann, Nancy. *The Intimate University: Korean American Students and the Problems of Segregation*. Durham: Duke University Press, 2009.

Abramson, Alan J., Lester M. Salamon, and C. Eugene Steuerle. "Federal Spending and Tax Policies: Their Implications for the Nonprofit Sector." In *Nonprofits and Government: Collaboration and Conflict*, edited by Elizabeth T. Boris and C. Eugene Steuerle, 107–40. Washington: Urban Institute Press, 2006.

Addams, Jane. *The Spirit of the Youth and the City Streets*. 1909. Champaign: University of Illinois Press, 1972.

Advancement Project and Civil Rights Project. *Opportunities Suspended: The Devastating Consequences of Zero Tolerance and School Discipline Policies*. Cambridge, MA: Harvard University, 2003.

Aguirre, Adalberto, and Shoon Lio. "Spaces of Mobilization: The Asian American/Pacific Islander Struggle for Social Justice." *Social Justice* 35, no. 2 (2008): 1–17.

Allen, Robert. "Black Awakening in Capitalist America." In *The Revolution Will Not Be Funded: Beyond the Non-Profit Industrial Complex*, edited by INCITE! Women of Color against Violence, 53–62. Cambridge, MA: South End, 2007.

Altbach, Philip. "Perspectives on Student Political Activism." In *Student Political Activism*, edited by Philip Altbach, 1–17. New York: Greenwood, 1989.

——. "Students and Politics." In *Student Politics*, edited by Seymour Martin Lipset, 74–93. New York: Basic Books, 1967.

Alvarez, Sonia E. "Advocating Feminism: The Latin American Feminist NGO 'Boom.'" *International Feminist Journal of Politics* 1, no. 2 (1999): 181–209.

——. "Beyond Ngo-ization? Reflections from Latin America." *Development* 52, no. 2 (2009): 175–84.

Arnove, Robert F., ed. *Philanthropy and Cultural Imperialism: The Foundations at Home and Abroad*. Boston: G. K. Hall, 1980.

Bennett, Stephen E. "Why Young Americans Hate Politics, and What We Should Do about It." *Political Science and Politics* 30, no. 1 (1997): 47–53.

Bennett, William J., Jr., John J. DiIulio, and John P. Walters. *Body Count: Moral Poverty and How to Win America's War against Crime and Drugs*. New York: Simon and Schuster, 1996.

Blaustein, Arthur, ed. *The American Promise: Equal Justice and Economic Opportunity*. New Brunswick, NJ: Transaction, 1982.

Boris, Elizabeth T. "Introduction—Nonprofit Organizations in a Democracy:

Varied Roles and Responsibilities." In *Nonprofits and Government: Collaboration and Conflict*, edited by Elizabeth T. Boris and C. Eugene Steuerle, 1–36. Washington: Urban Institute, 2006.

Brodkin, Karen. *Making Democracy Matter: Identity and Activism in Los Angeles.* New Brunswick, NJ: Rutgers University Press, 2007.

Brotherton, David C., and Philip Kretsedemas, eds. *Keeping Out the Other: A Critical Introduction to Immigration Enforcement Today.* New York: Columbia University Press, 2005.

Brown, Ruth Nicole. *Black Girlhood Celebration: Toward a Hip-Hop Feminist Pedagogy.* New York: Peter Lang, 2009.

Brown, Wendy. "Injury, Identity, Politics." In *Mapping Multiculturalism*, edited by Avery F. Gordon and Christopher Newfield, 149–66. Minneapolis: University of Minnesota Press, 1996.

———. "Neoliberalism and the End of Liberal Democracy." In Wendy Brown, *Edgework: Critical Essays on Knowledge and Politics*, 37–59. Princeton: Princeton University Press, 2005.

———. *States of Injury: Power and Freedom in Late Modernity.* Princeton: Princeton University Press, 1995.

Bryan, Mary Lynn McCree, and Allen F. Davis. "Beginnings: 1889–1900." In *100 Years at the Hull House*, edited by Mary Lynn McCree Bryan and Allen F. Davis, 1–10. Bloomington: Indiana University Press, 1990.

Bumiller, Kristin. *In an Abusive State: How Neoliberalism Appropriated the Feminist Movement against Sexual Violence.* Durham: Duke University Press, 2008.

Cacho, Lisa Marie. *Social Death: Racialized Rightlessness and the Criminalization of the Unprotected.* New York: New York University Press, 2012.

———. "'You Just Don't Know How Much He Meant': Deviancy, Death, and Devaluation." *Latino Studies* 5 (2007): 182–208.

Californians for Justice. *Still Separate, Still Unequal.* Oakland: Californians for Justice, 2001.

Cammarota, Julio, and Michelle Fine, eds. *Revolutionizing Education: Youth Participatory Action Research in Motion.* New York: Routledge, 2008.

Capps, Randy, Jacqueline Hagan, and Nestor Rodriguez. "Border Residents Manage the U.S. Immigration and Welfare Reforms." In *Immigrants, Welfare Reform, and the Poverty of Policy*, edited by Philip Kretsedemas and Ana Aparicio, 229–50. Westport, CT: Praeger, 2004.

Centers for Disease Control and Prevention. "Youth Risk Behavior Surveillance—United States 2005." Atlanta: Centers for Disease Control and Prevention, 2006.

Chandler, David. *A History of Cambodia.* Boulder: Westview, 2000.

———. *Voices from s-21: Terror and History in Pol Pot's Secret Prison.* Berkeley: University of California Press, 1999.

Chesney-Lind, Meda, and Lisa Pasko. *The Female Offender: Girls, Women, and Crime.* Thousand Oaks, CA: Sage, 2004.

Chesney-Lind, Meda, and Randall G. Shelden. *Girls, Delinquency, and Juvenile Justice.* Belmont, CA: West/Wadsworth, 2004.

Chuh, Kandice. *Imagine Otherwise*. Durham: Duke University Press, 2003.

Chung, Angie. *Legacies of Struggle: Conflict and Cooperation in Korean American Politics*. Stanford: Stanford University Press, 2007.

Clarke, John, et al. "Subcultures, Cultures, and Class." In *The Subcultures Reader*, edited by Ken Gelder and Sarah Thornton, 100–111. London: Routledge, 1997.

Cloward, Richard A., and Lloyd E. Ohlin. *Delinquency and Opportunity: A Theory of Delinquent Gangs*. Glencoe, IL: Free Press, 1960.

Cole, David. *Enemy Aliens: Double Standards and Constitutional Freedoms in the War on Terrorism*. New York: New Press, 2003.

Collins, Damien, and Robin Kearns. "Under Curfew and under Siege? Legal Geographies of Young People." *Geoforum* 32, no. 3 (2001): 389–403.

Comaroff, Jean, and John Comaroff. "Millennial Capitalism: First Thoughts on a Second Coming." *Public Culture* 12, no. 2 (2000): 291–343.

Cote, James E., and Anton L. Allahar. *Generation on Hold: Coming of Age in the Late Twentieth Century*. New York: New York University Press, 1994.

Coughlin, Brenda C. "Prison Walls Are Crumbling: The American Way of Punishment and Its Consequences." In *Youth, Globalization, and the Law*, edited by Sudhir Alladi Venkatesh and Ronald Kassimir, 192–222. Stanford: Stanford University Press, 2007.

Cruikshank, Barbara. *The Will to Empower: Democratic Citizens and Other Subjects*. Ithaca: Cornell University Press, 1999.

Das Gupta, Monisha. *Unruly Immigrants*. Durham: Duke University Press, 2006.

Davis, Allen. "Introduction." In Jane Addams, *The Spirit of the Youth and the City Streets*, vii–xxx. Champaign: University of Illinois Press, 1972.

DeGenova, Nicholas. "Migrant 'Illegality' and Deportability in Everyday Life." *Annual Review of Anthropology* 31 (2002): 419–47.

DeGenova, Nicholas, and Nathalie Peutz, eds. *The Deportation Regime: Sovereignty, Space, and the Freedom of Movement*. Durham: Duke University Press, 2010.

Delgado, Melvin, and Lee Staples. *Youth-Led Community Organizing: Theory and Action*. New York: Oxford University Press, 2008.

Diaz, Vincente M. "To 'P' or Not to 'P'? Marking the Territory between Pacific Islander and Asian American Studies." *Journal of Asian American Studies* 7, no. 3 (2004): 183–208.

Dolhinow, Rebecca. *A Jumble of Needs*. Minneapolis: University of Minnesota Press, 2010.

Dougherty, Mary, Denise Wilson, and Amy Wu. "Immigration Enforcement Actions: 2004." Washington: Department of Homeland Security, Office of Immigration Statistics, 2005.

Dow, Mark. *American Gulag: Inside U.S. Immigration Prisons*. Berkeley: University of California Press, 2004.

——. "Designed to Punish: Immigrant Detention and Deportation." *Social Research* 74, no. 2 (2007): 533–46.

Duggan, Lisa. *The Twilight of Equality: Neoliberalism, Cultural Politics, and the Attack of Democracy*. Boston: Beacon, 2003.

Eccles, Jacquelynne, and Jennifer Appleton-Gootman. *Community Programs to Promote Youth Development*. Washington: National Academies Press, 2002.

EdSource. *How California Ranks: A National Perspective*. Oakland, CA: EdSource, 2005.

Edwards, Ditra, Nicole Johnson, and Kim McGillicuddy. *An Emerging Model for Working with Youth: Community Organizing + Youth Development = Youth Organizing*. New York: Funders' Collaborative on Youth Organizing, 2003.

Edwards, Michael, and David Hulme, eds. *Non-Governmental Organisations—Performance and Accountability: Beyond the Magic Bullet*. London: Earthscan, 1995.

Eldredge, Sue, Sam Piha, and Jodi Levin. "Building the San Francisco Beacons." *New Directions for Youth Development* 2002, no. 94 (2002): 89–108.

Ellis, Susan, and Katherine H. Noyes. *By the People: A History of Americans as Volunteers*. San Francisco: Jossey-Bass, 1990.

Espiritu, Yen Le. *Asian American Panethnicity: Bridging Institutions and Identities*. Philadelphia: Temple University Press, 1992.

——. *Home Bound: Filipino American Lives across Culture, Communities, and Countries*. Berkeley: University of California Press, 2003.

Espiritu, Yen Le, and Michael Omi. "Who Are You Calling Asian? Shifting Identity Claims, Racial Classification, and the Census." In *Transforming Race Relations*, edited by Paul Ong, 43–101. Los Angeles: LEAP, Asian Pacific American Institute, and UCLA Asian American Center, 2000.

Farnam, Julie. *US Immigration Laws under the Threat of Terrorism*. New York: Algora, 2005.

Feld, Barry C. *Bad Kids: Race and the Transformation of the Juvenile Court*. New York: Oxford University Press, 1999.

——. "Girls in the Juvenile Justice System." In *The Delinquent Girl*, edited by Margaret A. Zahn, 225–64. Philadelphia: Temple University Press, 2009.

Ferguson, Ann. *Bad Boys: Public Schools in the Making of Black Masculinity*. Ann Arbor: University of Michigan Press, 2000.

Ferguson, Roderick. "Administering Sexuality; or, the Will to Institutionality." *Radical History Review* 100 (Winter 2008): 158–69.

Flanagan, Constance. "Volunteerism, Leadership, Political Socialization, and Civic Engagement." In *Handbook of Adolescent Psychology*, edited by Richard Lerner and Laurence Steinberg, 721–46. 2nd ed. New York: Wiley, 2004.

Flanagan, Constance, and Nakesha Faison. "Youth Civic Development: Implications of Research for Social Policy and Programs." *Social Policy Report* 15, no. 1 (2001): 3–15.

Foucault, Michel. *The Birth of Biopolitics: Lectures at the Collège de France 1978–1979*. Translated by Graham Burchell. New York: Palgrave Macmillan, 2008.

——. "Governmentality." In *The Foucault Effect: Studies in Governmentality*, edited by Graham Burchell, Colin Gordon, and Peter Miller. Chicago: University of Chicago Press, 1991.

Fraser, Nancy. *Justice Interruptus: Critical Reflections on the "Post Socialist" Condition*. New York: Routledge, 1997.

Freeman, Gary. "Client Politics or Populism? Immigration Reform in the United States." In *Controlling a New Migration World*, edited by Virginie Guiraudon and Christian Joppke, 65–96. London: Routledge, 2001.

Fulbright-Anderson, Karen, et al. *Structural Racism and Youth Development: Issues, Challenges, and Implications*. Washington: Aspen Institute, 2005.

Galaskiewicz, Joseph, and Wolfgang Bielefeld. *Nonprofit Organizations in an Age of Uncertainty: A Study of Organizational Change*. New York: Aldine De Gruyter, 1998.

Gans, Herbert. *The War against the Poor: The Underclass and Antipoverty Policy*. New York: Basic Books, 1995.

Ganz, Marshall. "Resources and Resourcefulness: Strategic Capacity in the Unionization of California Agriculture." *American Journal of Sociology* 105, no. 4 (2000): 1003–62.

Geertz, Clifford. *The Interpretation of Cultures*. New York: Basic Books, 1973.

Geron, Kim. "Serve the People: An Exploration of the Asian American Movement." In *Asian American Politics: Law, Participation, and Policy*, edited by Don Nakanishi and James Lai, 163–79. Lanham, MD: Rowman and Littlefield, 2003.

Gilmore, Ruth Wilson. *Golden Gulag: Prisons Surplus, Crisis, and Opposition in Globalizing California*. Berkeley: University of California Press, 2007.

——. "In the Shadow of the Shadow State." In *The Revolution Will Not Be Funded: Beyond the Non-Profit Industrial Complex*, edited by INCITE! Women of Color against Violence, 41–52. Cambridge, MA: South End, 2007.

Ginwright, Shawn. *Building a Pipeline for Justice: Understanding Youth Organizing and the Leadership Pipeline*. New York: Funders' Collaborative on Youth Organizing, 2010.

——. *Youth Organizing: Expanding Possibilities for Youth Development*. New York: Funders' Collaborative on Youth Organizing, 2003.

Ginwright, Shawn, and Taj James. "From Assets to Agents of Change: Social Justice, Organizing, and Youth Development." *New Direction for Youth Development* 2002, no. 96 (Winter 2002): 27–46.

Ginwright, Shawn, Pedro Noguera, and Julio Cammarota, eds. *Beyond Resistance! Youth Activism and Community Change*. New York: Routledge, 2006.

Glassner, Barry. *The Culture of Fear: Why Americans Are Afraid of the Wrong Things*. New York: Basic Books, 2000.

Gordon, Avery F., and Christopher Newfield. "Multiculturalism's Unfinished Business." In *Mapping Multiculturalism*, edited by Avery F. Gordon and Christopher Newfield, 76–115. Minneapolis: University of Minnesota Press, 1996.

Gordon, Colin. "Governmental Rationality: An Introduction." In *The Foucault Effect: Studies in Governmentality*, edited by Graham Burchell, Colin Gordon, and Peter Miller, 1–52. Chicago: University of Chicago Press, 1991.

Gordon, Hava Rachel. *We Fight to Win: Inequality and the Politics of Youth Activism*. New Brunswick, NJ: Rutgers University Press, 2010.

Gordon, Linda. "Southeast Asian Refugee Migration to the United States." In *Pacific Bridges: The New Immigration from Asia and the Pacific Islands*, edited by James T. Fawcett and Benjamin V. Carino, 153–73. Staten Island, NY: Center for Migration Studies, 1987.

Gramsci, Antonio. *Selections from the Prison Notebooks of Antonio Gramsci*. Translated and edited by Quintin Hoare and Geoffrey Nowell Smith. New York: International, 1999.

Grewal, Inderpal. *Transnational America: Feminisms, Diasporas, Neoliberalisms*. Durham: Duke University Press, 2005.

Griffin, Christine. *Representations of Youth: The Study of Youth and Adolescence in Britain and America*. Cambridge: Polity, 1993.

Gronbjerg, Kristen A., and Lester M. Salamon. "Devolution, Marketization, and the Changing Shape of Government-Nonprofit Relations." In *The State of Nonprofit America*, edited by Lester M. Salamon. 447–70. Washington: Brookings Institution, 2002.

Guerrero, Michael Leon. "You Can't Spell Fundraising without F-U-N: The Resource Mob, the Non-Profit Industrial Complex, and the USSF." In *The United States Social Forum: Perspectives of a Movement*, edited by Marina Karides et al., 61–76. Chicago: Changemaker, 2010.

Habal, Estella. *San Francisco's International Hotel: Mobilizing the Filipino American Community in the Anti-Eviction Movement*. Philadelphia: Temple University Press, 2008.

Hagan, Frank E. *Introduction to Criminology: Theories, Methods, and Criminal Behavior*. Thousand Oaks, CA: Sage, 2008.

Hale, Charles, ed. *Engaging Contradictions, Theory, Politics, and Methods of Activist Scholarship*. Berkeley: University of California Press, 2008.

Hall, G. Stanley. *Adolescence: Its Psychology and Its Relations to Physiology, Anthropology, Sociology, Sex, Crime, and Religion, Volume I*. 1904. New York: D. Appleton, 1931.

Hall, Stuart. "Gramsci's Relevance for the Study of Race and Ethnicity." *Journal of Communication Inquiry* 10, no. 5 (1986): 5–27.

Halpern, Robert. "A Different Kind of Child Development Institution: The History of After-School Programs for Low-Income Children." *Teachers College Review* 104, no. 2 (2002): 178–211.

——. *Making Play Work: The Promise of After-School Programs for Low-Income Children*. New York: Teachers College Press, 2003.

Harder, Paul, James Musselwhite Jr., and Lester Salamon. *Government Spending and the Nonprofit Sector in San Francisco*. Washington: Urban Institute, 1984.

Harrison, Anthony Kwame. *Hip Hop Underground: The Integrity and Ethics of Racial Identification*. Philadelphia: Temple University Press, 2001.

Hartney, Christopher, and Fabiana Silva. *And Justice for Some: Differential Treatment of Youth of Color in the Justice System*. Oakland, CA: National Council on Crime and Delinquency, 2007.

Harvey, David. *A Brief History of Neoliberalism*. Oxford: Oxford University Press, 2005.

Hawk, Madonna Thunder. "Native Organizing before the Non-Profit Industrial

Complex." In *The Revolution Will Not Be Funded: Beyond the Non-Profit Industrial Complex*, edited by INCITE! Women of Color against Violence, 101–6. Cambridge, MA: South End, 2007.

Hebdige, Dick. *Subculture: The Meaning of Style*. London: Routledge, 1979.

Hein, Jeremy. *From Vietnam, Laos, and Cambodia: A Refugee Experience in the United States*. New York: Twayne, 1995.

Hing, Bill Ong. "Deporting Cambodian Refugees: Justice Denied?" *Crime and Delinquency* 51, no. 2 (2005): 265–90.

Hinton, Alexander Laban. *Why Did They Kill? Cambodia in the Shadow of Genocide*. Berkeley: University of California Press, 2005.

Hodgkinson, Virgina. "Individual Giving and Volunteering." In *The State of Nonprofit America*, edited by Lester M. Salamon, 387–420. Washington: Brookings Institution, 2002.

HoSang, Daniel. *Traditions and Innovations: Youth Organizing in the Southwest*. New York: Funders' Collaborative on Youth Organizing, 2005.

———. *Youth and Community Organizing*. New York: Funders' Collaborative on Youth Organizing, 2003.

INCITE! Women of Color against Violence, ed. *The Revolution Will Not Be Funded: Beyond the Non-Profit Industrial Complex*. Cambridge, MA: South End, 2007.

Irby, Merita, Thaddeus Ferber, and Karen Pittman. *Youth Action, Youth Contributing to Communities, Communities Supporting Youth*. Washington: Forum for Youth Investment, Impact Strategies, 2001.

Ishihara, Kohei. *Urban Transformations: Youth Organizing in Boston, New York City, Philadelphia, and Washington D.C.* New York: Funder's Collaborative on Youth Organizing, 2007.

Jarrett, Robin, Patrick Sullivan, and Natasha Wilkens. "Developing Social Capital through Participation in Organized Youth Programs: Qualitative Insights from Three Programs." *Journal of Community Psychology* 33, no. 1 (2005): 41–55.

Jennings, Kent, and Richard Niemi. *The Political Character of Adolescence: The Influence of Families and Schools*. Princeton: Princeton University Press, 1974.

Joseph, Miranda. *Against the Romance of Community*. Minneapolis: University of Minnesota Press, 2002.

Juris, Jeffery. "Social Forums and Their Margins: Networking Logics and the Cultural Politics of Autonomous Space." *ephemera* 5, no. 2 (2005): 253–72.

Karim, Lamia. *Microfinance and Its Discontents: Women in Debt in Bangladesh*. Minneapolis: University of Minnesota Press, 2011.

Kauanui, J. Kehaulani. "Asian American Studies and the 'Pacific Question.'" In *Asian American Studies after Critical Mass*, edited by Kent Ono, 123–43. Malden, MA: Blackwell, 2005.

Kennedy, Angie C. "Eugenics, 'Degenerate Girls,' and Social Workers during the Progressive Era." *Affilia* 23, no. 1 (2008): 22–37.

Kibria, Nazli. *Becoming Asian American: Second-Generation Chinese and Korean American Identities*. Baltimore: Johns Hopkins University Press, 2002.

Kim, Claire Jean. "Asian Americans Are People of Color, Too . . . Aren't They?" *aapi nexus* 2, no. 1 (2004): 19–47.

Kirshner, Benjamin. "Power in Numbers: Youth Organizing as a Context for Exploring Civic Identity." *Journal of Research on Adolescence* 19, no. 3 (2008): 414–40.

Krisberg, Barry, and James Austin. *Reinventing Juvenile Justice.* Newbury Park, CA: Sage Publications, 1993.

Kwon, Soo Ah. "Autoexoticizing: Asian American Youth and the Import Scene." *Journal of Asian American Studies* 7, no. 1 (2004): 1–26.

——. "Moving from Complaints to Action: Oppositional Consciousness and Collective Action in a Political Community." *Anthropology and Education Quarterly* 39, no. 1 (2008): 59–76.

——. "The Institutionalization of a Panethnic Identity." *Journal of Asian American Studies*, forthcoming.

Lanier, Mark, and Stuart Henry. *Essentialist Criminology.* Boulder: Westview, 2004.

Larson, Kate Gifford. "The Saturday Evening Girls: A Progressive Era Library Club and the Intellectual Life of Working Class and Immigrant Girls in Turn-of-the-Century Boston." *Library Quarterly* 71, no. 2 (2001): 195–230.

Larson, Reed, and David Hansen. "The Development of Strategic Thinking: Learning to Impact Human Systems in a Youth Activism Program." *Human Development* 48 (2005): 327–49.

Larson, Reed, et al. "Organized Youth Activities as Contexts for Positive Development." In *Positive Psychology in Practice*, edited by P. Alex Linley and Stephen Joseph, 540–60. New York: Wiley, 2004.

Lashaw, Amanda. "The Presence of Hope in a Movement for Equitable Schooling." *Space and Culture* 11, no. 2 (2008): 109–24.

Le, Thao. "Delinquency among Asian/Pacific Islanders: Review of Literature and Research." *Justice Professional* 15 (2002): 57–70.

Le, Thao, et al. *Not Invisible: Asian Pacific Islander Juvenile Arrests in Alameda County.* Oakland, CA: National Council on Crime and Delinquency, 2001.

——. *Not Invisible: Asian Pacific Islander Juvenile Arrests in San Francisco County.* Oakland, CA: National Council on Crime and Delinquency, 2001.

Lee, Jennifer, and Min Zhou. *Asian American Youth: Culture, Identity, and Ethnicity.* New York: Routledge, 2004.

Lee, Stacey J. *Unraveling the "Model Minority" Stereotype: Listening to Asian American Youth.* New York: Teachers College Press, 1996.

——. *Up against Whiteness: Race, School, and Immigrant Youth.* New York: Teachers College Press, 2005.

Lesko, Nancy. "Denaturalizing Adolescence: The Politics of Contemporary Representations." *Youth and Society* 28, no. 2 (1996): 139–61.

Levine, Peter, and James Youniss, eds. *Youth Civic Engagement: An Institutional Turn.* Medford, MA: Center for Information and Research on Civic Learning and Engagement, Tufts University, 2006.

Levitt, Cyril. *Children of Privilege: Student Revolt in the Sixties; A Study of Student Movements in Canada, the United States, and West Germany*. Toronto: University of Toronto Press, 1984.

Li, Tania Murray. *The Will to Improve: Governmentality, Development, and the Practice of Politics*. Durham: Duke University Press, 2007.

Livingston, Steven Greene. *Student's Guide to Landmark Congressional Laws on Social Security and Welfare*. Westport, CT: Greenwood, 2002.

Loescher, Gil, and John A. Scanlan. *Calculated Kindness: Refugees and America's Half-Open Door, 1945 to the Present*. New York: Simon and Schuster, 1998.

Lowe, Lisa. *Immigrant Acts: On Asian American Cultural Politics*. Durham: Duke University Press, 1996.

Lubeck, Sally, and Patricia Garrett. "The Social Construction of the 'At-Risk' Child." *British Journal of Sociology of Education* 11, no. 3 (1990): 327–40.

Luker, Kristin. *Dubious Conceptions: The Politics of Teenage Pregnancy*. Cambridge, MA: Harvard University Press, 1996.

Ma, L. Eve Armentrout. *Hometown Chinatown: The History of Oakland's Chinese Community*. New York: Garland, 2000.

Maira, Sunaina. "Deporting Radicals, Deporting *La Migra*." *Cultural Text* 19, no. 1 (2007): 39–66.

——. *Desis in the House*. Philadelphia: Temple University Press, 2002.

——. *Missing: Youth, Citizenship, and Empire after 9/11*. Durham: Duke University Press, 2009.

Males, Mike A. *Framing Youth: Ten Myths about the Next Generation*. Monroe, ME: Common Courage, 1999.

——. *The Scapegoat Generation: America's War on Adolescents*. Monroe, ME: Common Courage, 1996.

Mann, Sheilah. "What the Survey of American College Freshmen Tells Us about Their Interest in Politics and Political Science." *Political Science and Politics* 32, no. 2 (1999): 263–68.

Mansbridge, Jane J. *Beyond Adversary Democracy*. Chicago: University of Chicago Press, 1983.

Marable, Manning. *Race, Reform, and Rebellion: The Second Reconstruction in Black America*. Jackson: University Press of Mississippi, 1991.

McAdam, Doug. *Political Process and the Development of Black Insurgency, 1930–1970*. 2nd ed. Chicago: University of Chicago Press, 1982.

McLaughlin, Milbrey, Merita A. Irby, and Juliet Langman. *Urban Sanctuaries: Neighborhood Organizations in the Lives and Futures of Inner-City Youth*. San Francisco: Jossey-Bas, 1994.

Meiners, Erica. *Right to Be Hostile: Schools, Prisons, and the Making of Public Enemies*. New York: Routledge, 2007.

Melamed, Jodi. "The Spirit of Neoliberalism: From Racial Liberalism to Neoliberal Multiculturalism." *Social Text* 24, no. 4 (2006): 1–24.

Min, Pyong Gap. *The Second Generation: Ethnic Identity among Asian Americans*. Walnut Creek, CA: Alta Mira, 2002.

Min, Pyong Gap, and Kyeyong Park, eds. "Second Generation Asian Americans' Ethnic Identity." Special issue, *amerasia* 25, no. 1 (1999).

Mindry, Debra. "Nongovernmental Organizations, 'Grassroots,' and the Politics of Virtue." *Signs* 26, no. 4 (2001): 1187–211.

Mitchell, Katharyne. "Pre-Black Futures." *Antipode* 41 (2009): 239–61.

Mohanty, Chandra Talpade. "On Race and Voice: Challenges for Liberal Education in the 1990s." In *Beyond a Dream Deferred: Multicultural Education and the Politics of Excellence*, edited by Becky Thompson and Sangeeta Tyagi, 41–65. Minneapolis: University of Minnesota Press, 1993.

Morawetz, Nancy. "Rethinking Retroactive Deportation Laws and the Due Process Clause." *New York University Law Review* 73 (1998): 97–161.

——. "Understanding the Impact of the 1996 Deportation Laws and the Limited Scope of Proposed Reforms." *Harvard Law Review* 113, no. 1936 (2000): 1–22.

Morris, Aldon D. *Origins of the Civil Rights Movement: Black Communities Organizing for Change*. New York: Free Press, 1984.

Muncie, John, and Gordon Hughes. "Modes of Youth Governance: Political Rationalities, Original and Resistance." In *Youth Justice Critical Readings*, edited by John Muncie, Gordon Hughes, and Eugene McLaughlin, 1–18. London: Sage, 2002.

Naber, Nadine. "The Rules of Forced Engagement: Race, Gender, and the Culture of Fear among Arab Immigrants in San Francisco Post-9/11." *Cultural Dynamics* 18, no. 3 (2006): 235–67.

——. "So Our History Doesn't Become Your Future: The Local and Global Politics of Coalition Building Post September 11th." *Journal of Asian American Studies* 5, no. 3 (2002): 217–42.

Nathanson, Constance. *Dangerous Passage: The Social Control of Sexuality in Women's Adolescence*. Philadelphia: Temple University Press, 1991.

Ngô, Fiona I. B., Mimi Thi Nguyen, and Mariam B. Lam. "Southeast Asian American Studies." Special issue, *positions* 20, no. 3 (2012).

Nguyen, Mimi Thi. *The Gift of Freedom: War, Debt, and Other Refugee Passages*. Durham: Duke University Press, 2012.

Nishida, Mori. "Serve the People." In *Asian Americans: The Movement and the Moment*, edited by Steve Louie and Glenn Omatsu, 305–6. Los Angeles: UCLA Asian American Studies Center Press, 2006.

O'Connor, Alice. "Community Action, Urban Reform, and the Fight against Poverty: The Ford Foundation's Gray Areas Program." *Journal of Urban History* 22, no. 5 (1996): 586–625.

Odem, Mary. *Delinquent Daughters: Protecting and Policing Adolescent Female Sexuality in the United States 1885–1920*. Chapel Hill: University of North Carolina Press, 1995.

Office of Juvenile Justice and Delinquency Prevention. *Juvenile Justice: A Century of Change*. Washington: Department of Justice, 1999.

Omi, Michael, and Howard Winant. *Racial Formation in the United States: From the 1960s to the 1990s*. 2nd ed. New York: Routledge, 1994.

O'Neill, Michael. *The Third America*. San Francisco: Jossey-Bass, 1989.

Ong, Aihwa. *Buddha Is Hiding: Refugees, Citizenship, and the New America*. Berkeley: University of California Press, 2003.

Ong, Paul, and John M. Liu. "U.S. Immigration Policies and Asia Migration." In *The New Asian Immigration in Los Angeles and Global Restructuring*, edited by Paul Ong, Edna Bonacich, and Lucie Cheng, 45–73. Philadelphia: Temple University Press, 1994.

Palumbo-Liu, David. *Asian/American: Historical Crossings of a Racial Frontier*. Stanford: Stanford University Press, 1999.

Park, Edward, and John Park. *Probationary Americans*. New York: Routledge, 2005.

Pateman, Carole. *Participation and Democratic Theory*. Cambridge: Cambridge University Press, 1970.

Patton, Cindy. "Refiguring Social Space." In *Social Postmodernism: Beyond Identity Politics*, edited by Linda Nicholson and Steven Seidman, 216–49. Cambridge: Cambridge University Press, 1995.

Peck, Jamie. *Workfare States*. New York: Guilford, 2001.

Pierson, Paul. *Dismantling the Welfare State? Reagan, Thatcher, and the Politics of Retrenchment*. Cambridge: Cambridge University Press, 1994.

Pintado-Vertner, Ryan. *The West Coast Story: The Emergence of Youth Organizing in California*. New York: Funders' Collaborative on Youth Organizing, 2004.

Pittman, Karen, and Merita A. Irby. *An Advocate's Guide to Youth Development*. Washington: Center for Youth Development and Policy Research, 1995.

Pittman, Karen, and Marlene Wright. *Bridging the Gap: A Rationale for Enhancing the Role of Community Organizations in Promoting Youth Development*. Washington: Carnegie Council on Adolescent Development, 1991.

Pittman, Karen, et al. *Preventing Problems, Promoting Development, Encouraging Engagement: Competing Priorities or Inseparable Goals*. Washington: Forum for Youth Investment, Impact Strategies, 2003.

Piven, Frances Fox, and Richard A. Cloward. *Poor People's Movements: Why They Succeed, How They Fail*. New York: Vintage, 1979.

Platt, Anthony. *The Child Savers: The Invention of Delinquency*. Chicago: University of Chicago Press, 1977.

——. "The Triumph of Benevolence: The Origins of the Juvenile Justice System in the United States." In *Criminal Justice in America*, edited by Richard Quinney, 356–89. Boston: Little, Brown, 1974.

Proietto, Rosa. "The Ford Foundation and Women's Studies in Media Higher Education: Seeds of Change?" In *Philanthropic Foundations: New Scholarship, New Possibilities*, edited by Ellen Condliffe Lagemann, 271–86. Bloomington: Indiana University Press, 1999.

Pulido, Laura. *Black, Brown, Yellow and Left: Radical Activism in Los Angeles*. Berkeley: University of California Press, 2006.

——. "Development of the 'People of Color' Identity in the Environmental Justice Movement of the Southwestern United States." *Socialist Review* 26 (1996): 145–80.

Pyke, Karen, and Tran Dang. "'Fob' and 'Whitewashed': Identity and Internalized Racism among Second Generation Asian Americans." *Qualitative Sociology* 26, no. 2 (2003): 147–72.

Regal, J. M. *Oakland's Partnership for Change*. Oakland, CA: Department of Human Resources, 1967.

Rhomberg, Chris. *No There There: Race, Class, and Political Community in Oakland*. Berkeley: University of California Press, 2004.

Rodriguez, Dylan. "Asian-American Studies in the Age of the Prison Industrial Complex: Departures and Re-Narrations." *Review of Education, Pedagogy, and Cultural Studies* 27, no. 3 (2005): 241–63.

——. "The Political Logic of the Non-Profit Industrial Complex." In *The Revolution Will Not Be Funded: Beyond the Non-Profit Industrial Complex*, edited by INCITE! Women of Color against Violence, 21–40. Cambridge, MA: South End, 2007.

Rodriguez, Robyn, and Nerissa S. Balce. "American Insecurity and Radical Filipino Community Politics." *Peace Review* 16, no. 2 (2004): 131–40.

Roediger, David. *Working toward Whiteness: How America's Immigrants Became White*. New York: Basic Books, 2005.

Rose, Nikolas. "The Death of the Social? Re-Figuring the Territory of the Government." *Economy and Society* 25, no. 3 (1996): 327–56.

——. *Governing the Soul: The Shaping of the Private Self*. London: Free Association, 1989.

Ross, Andrew, and Tricia Rose, eds. *Microphone Fiends: Youth Music and Youth Culture*. New York: Routledge, 1994.

Rudrappa, Sharmila. *Ethnic Routes to Becoming American*. Minneapolis: University of Minnesota Press, 2004.

Salamon, Lester M. "The Resilient Sector: The State of Nonprofit America." In *The State of Nonprofit America*, edited by Lester M. Salamon, 3–61. Washington: Brookings Institution, 2002.

Sanford, Victoria, and Asale Angel-Ajani, eds. *Engaged Observer: Anthropology, Advocacy, and Activism*. New Brunswick, NJ: Rutgers University Press, 2006.

Schwartz, Ira M. *(In)Justice for Juveniles: Rethinking the Best Interests of the Child*. Lexington, MA: Lexington Books, 1989.

Self, Robert. *American Babylon: Race and the Struggle for Postwar Oakland*. Princeton: Princeton University Press, 2003.

Seng, Jana M. "Cambodian Nationality Law and the Repatriation of Convicted Aliens under the Illegal Immigration Reform and Immigrant Responsibility Act." *Pacific Rim Law and Policy Journal* 10, no. 2 (2001): 443–69.

Shah, Seema. *Building Transformative Youth Leadership: Data on the Impacts of Youth Organizing*. New York: Funders' Collaborative on Youth Organizing, 2011.

Shahidullah, Shahid M. *Crime Policy in America: Law, Institutions, and Programs*. Lanham, MD: University Press of America, 2008.

Shankar, Shalini. *Desi Land: Teen Culture, Class, and Success in Silicon Valley*. Durham: Duke University Press, 2008.

Sharma, Aradhana. *Logics of Empowerment: Development, Gender, and Governance in Neoliberal India*. Minneapolis: University of Minnesota Press, 2008.

Sharma, Nitasha. *Hip Hop Desis: South Asian Americans, Blackness, and a Global Race Consciousness*. Durham: Duke University Press, 2010.

Shelden, Randall G. *Detention Diversion Advocacy: An Evaluation*. Washington: Department of Justice, 1999.

Shiao, Jay. *Identifying Talent, Institutionalizing Diversity: Race and Philanthropy in Post–Civil Rights America*. Durham: Duke University Press, 2005.

Shuck, Peter. *Citizens, Strangers, and In-Betweens: Essays on Immigration and Citizenship*. Boulder, CO: Westview, 1988.

Simanski, John, and Lesley M. Sapp. *Immigration Enforcement Actions: 2011*. Washington: Department of Homeland Security Office of Immigration Statistics, 2012.

Smith, Andrea. "Heteropatriarchy and the Three Pillars of White Supremacy: Rethinking Women of Color Organizing." In *Color of Violence: The INCITE! Anthology*, edited by INCITE! Women of Color against Violence, 66–73. Cambridge, MA: South End, 2006.

——. "Introduction: The Revolution Will Not Be Funded." In *The Revolution Will Not Be Funded: Beyond the Non-Profit Industrial Complex*, edited by INCITE! Women of Color against Violence, 1–20. Cambridge, MA: South End, 2007.

——. *Native Americans and the Christian Right: The Gendered Politics of Unlikely Alliances*. Durham: Duke University Press, 2008.

Smith, Steven Rathgeb, and Michael Lipsky. *Nonprofits for Hire: The Welfare State in the Age of Contracting*. Cambridge, MA: Harvard University Press, 1993.

Spade, Dean. *Normal Life: Administrative Violence, Critical Trans Politics and the Limits of Law*. Cambridge, MA: South End, 2011.

Sullivan, Lisa. "The State of Youth Organizing: 1990–2000." *State of Philanthropy* (2002): 25–30.

Tait, Vanessa. *Poor Workers' Unions: Rebuilding Labor from Below*. Cambridge, MA: South End, 2005.

Tang, Eric, and Harmony Goldberg. *The Funders' Collaborative on Youth Organizing's Roots Initiative Toolkit*. New York: Funders' Collaborative on Youth Organizing, 2007.

Task Force on Youth Development and Community Programs, Carnegie Council on Adolescent Development. *A Matter of Time: Risk and Opportunity in the Nonschool Hours*. Washington: Carnegie Council on Adolescent Development, 1992.

Taylor, Margaret. "*Demore v. Kim*: Judicial Deference to Congressional Folly." In *Immigration Stories*, edited by David A. Martin and Peter H. Schuck, 343–76. New York: Foundation, 2005.

Tilton, Jennifer. *Dangerous or Endangered*. New York: New York University Press, 2010.

Toribo, Helen. "The Problematics of History and Location of Filipino American Studies within Asian American Studies." In *Asian American Studies after Critical Mass*, edited by Kent Ono, 166–76. Malden, MA: Blackwell, 2005.

Torres-Fleming, Alexie, Pilar Valdes, and Supriya Pillai. *2010 Youth Organizing Field Scan*. New York: Funders' Collaborative on Youth Organizing, 2010.

Ung, Loung. *First They Killed My Father: A Daughter of Cambodia Remembers*. New York: HarperCollins, 2000.

US Bureau of the Census. "Summary File 1 (SF1) 100-Percent Data." Census 2000. Washington: Bureau of the Census, 2001.

———. "Summary File 2 (SF2) 100-Percent Data." Census 2000. Washington: Bureau of the Census, 2001.

Viorst, Milton. *The Citizen Poor of the 1960's: An Examination into a Social Experiment*. Dayton, OH: Charles F. Kettering Foundation, 1977.

Võ, Linda Trinh. *Mobilizing an Asian American Community*. Philadelphia: Temple University Press, 2004.

Volpp, Leti. "The Citizen and the Terrorist." In *September 11 in History: A Watershed Moment?*, edited by Mary L. Dudziak, 147–62. Durham: Duke University Press, 2003.

Wallace, Nicole. "Foundations Putting Money into Campaigns Led by Youths." *Chronicle of Philanthropy* 15, no. 6 (2003): 11.

Walter Leitner International Human Rights Clinic, Returnee Integration Support Center, and Deported Diaspora. *Removing Refugees: U.S. Deportation Policy and the Cambodian-American Community*. New York: Leitner Center for International Law and Justice at Fordham Law School, 2010.

Walzer, Michael. *Obligations: Essays on Disobedience, War, and Citizenship*. Cambridge, MA: Harvard University Press, 1970.

Watts, Roderick J., and Constance Flanagan. "Pushing the Envelope on Youth Civic Engagement: A Developmental and Liberation Psychology Perspective." *Journal of Community Psychology* 35, no. 6 (2007): 779–92.

Watts, Roderick J., and Omar Guessous. "Sociopolitical Development: The Missing Link in Research and Policy on Adolescents." In *Beyond Resistance! Youth Activism and Community Change*, edited by Shawn Ginwright, Pedro Noguera, and Julio Cammarota, 59–80. New York: Routledge, 2006.

Wei, William. *The Asian American Movement*. Philadelphia: Temple University Press, 1993.

Weiss, Mattie. *Youth Rising*. Oakland, CA: Applied Research Center, 2003.

Wordes, Madeline, Barry Krisberg, and Giselle Barry. *Facing the Future: Juvenile Detention in Alameda County*. Oakland, CA: National Council on Crime and Delinquency, 2001.

Yee, Sylvia. "Developing the Field of Youth Organizing and Advocacy: What Foundations Can Do." In "Community Organizing and Youth Advocacy," edited by Sarah Deschenes, Milbrey McLaughlin, and Anne Newman, special issue, *New Directions for Youth Development* 2002, no. 117 (2008): 109–24.

Youniss, James, et al. "Youth Civic Engagement in the Twenty-First Century." *Journal of Research on Adolescence* 12, no. 1 (2002): 121–48.

Zilberg, Elana. "Refugee Gang Youth: Zero Tolerance and the Security State in Contemporary U.S.-Salvadoran Relations." In *Youth, Globalization, and the*

Law, edited by Sudhir Alladi Venkatesh and Ronald Kassimir, 61–89. Stanford: Stanford University Press, 2007.

Zimring, Franklin. *American Juvenile Justice*. Oxford: Oxford University Press, 2005.

——. *American Youth Violence*. Oxford: Oxford University Press, 1998.

INDEX

Addams, Jane, 30–31, 32–33, 34
Adolescence: Its Psychology and Its Relations to Physiology, Anthropology, Sociology, Sex, Crime, and Religion (Hall), 29
affirmative governmentality, 9; community responsibility in, 56–58; self-empowerment strategies, 12, 55–56, 126; and youth organizing, 10–11, 119
African Americans: black nationalism and philanthropic funding, 63–64; gendered criminalization of, 41–43; youth incarceration, 79; zero-tolerance policies on, 83
after-school programs, 31, 33; Measure K (the Kids First! Initiative), 1, 11, 45, 133n34; Progressive Era reforms, 8, 27, 30, 31, 33
Anti-Terrorism and Effective Death Penalty Act, 96–97, 98, 145n3
Arab Americans, coalitions with Asian Americans, 118
Asian Americans: model minority myth, 84–85, 87–88; professionalization of community organizations, 59–60
Asian/Pacific Islander Youth Promoting Advocacy and Leadership (AYPAL), 1; drug and violence prevention workshops, 69–70; formation and structure of, 22–24; IIRIRA activism, 101–6, 115–16; methods, 20–21, 24–25; panethnic organizing within, 91–93, 94; racialization of members, 90–91. *See also* Stop the Super Jail campaign

"at-risk" youth: construct of, 4, 7–9, 46–47; criminalization, 80; funding for, 52, 54–55; managing via empowerment, 11, 47–50, 119; role of nonprofit organizations, 58, 69–70

Black Panthers, 77, 92
Books Not Bars Project, 76–77
Brown, Ruth Nicole, 72
Brown, Wendy, 60, 119, 132n26, 132n28
Bush administration, President George H. W., 19
Bush administration, President George W., 19, 99–100

Cacho, Lisa Marie, 8
California: community organizing, 2–3; criminal-law production in, 40; Proposition 21, 2, 3, 7; Proposition 187, 2, 98; resources for incarceration versus education, 81–83; youth delinquency data, 41–42; youth detention capacity, 78–79 (*see also* Stop the Super Jail campaign). *See also* Oakland
Californians for Justice, 2
Cambodian deportations, 96–97, 99–100; accounts of, 95, 100, 107–9; impact on refugee deportees, 110; Southeast Asian Freedom Network, 103
Cambodian refugees, 110–12
Carnegie Council on Adolescent Development 1992 report, 11–12, 45, 46–48
Centers for Disease Control and Prevention, 47–48

citizenship: under neoliberalism, 9–10; and political practices, 17–20, 107, 147n35
citizen-subjects, 8–9, 48, 97, 101, 107, 128
Civil Rights Act, 141n61
civil society: as governmental technology, 9, 71, 125, 126–27; nonprofit organizations in, 13–14, 58 (*see also* nonprofit organizations); and state, 5, 12–13, 15
Clinton administration, policies under, 57, 78. *See also* Illegal Immigration Reform and Immigrant Responsibility Act
Cloward, Richard, 49
community policing, 57–58
criminalization. *See* youth criminalization
Cruikshank, Barbara, 11, 29, 128, 133n38

delinquency. *See* youth delinquency
deportation: agreements with Southeast Asian countries, 99–100; of criminal aliens, 96–97, 98, 99; as state power, 99, 112–14, 118–19
detention centers, 108–9
DiIulio, John, 41, 138n61

Economic Opportunity Act (1964), 49, 141n61
education versus resources for youth incarceration, 81–83
Edward W. Hazen Foundation, 52, 53
empowerment, 11–12, 133n38
Espiritu, Yen Le, 59, 63–64
Evelyn and Walter Haas Jr. Fund, 11, 45, 50, 52, 56

federal grant programs: for Asian and Pacific Islander communities, 22, 59; contracting for services, 61–62; "kid-fixing" programs, 44, 47–48; retrenching of, 59–61
Feld, Barry, 42

Ferguson, Roderick, 64
Filipinos, deportation of, 116
501(c)(3) nonprofit organizations, 59. *See also* nonprofit organizations
Ford Foundation: Community Youth Development Initiative, 50; Gray Areas Programs, 48–49, 139–40nn9–10; intervention in civil rights struggle, 63
Foucault, Michel: governmentality, 9–10, 128–29, 132n23; on social policy under neoliberalism, 56
Funders' Collaborative for Youth Organizing (FCYO): formation of, 53–54; Regenerations: Leadership Pipeline initiative, 66, 123–25, 147n1

Gang Violence and Juvenile Crime Prevention Act. *See* Proposition 21
Gilmore, Ruth Wilson, 40
governmentality: Foucauldian concept of, 9–10, 128–29; voluntary participation of marginalized groups, 56–57. *See also* affirmative governmentality
Gramsci, Antonio, 13, 128, 129
Gray Areas Programs (Ford Foundation), 48–49, 139–40nn9–10
Great Society social programs, 13, 59, 61, 133n38
Gun-Free Schools Act (1994), 83

Hall, Stanley G., 29, 136n6
Hall, Stuart, 13, 129
Halpern, Robert, 8, 30, 33, 61
Harvey, David, 13
hip-hop, as protest, 77
Hull House: activities at, 30–31; Americanization project at, 33; support for, 32, 137n21

Illegal Immigration Reform and Immigrant Responsibility Act (1996), 96–97, 98, 145n3; youth activism against, 101–6

Illinois juvenile court act (1899), 37, 136n1
Immigration and Nationality Act (1965), 23
In re Gault (1967), 41
Irby, Merita, 50

Johnson administration, policies under, 46, 59
Joseph, Miranda, 56, 62
juvenile court and justice system: creation of, 27, 31–32, 136n1; juvenile delinquency construct in, 36–39; trends, 40–45. *See also* Progressive Era reform
juvenile delinquency. *See* youth delinquency
Juvenile Delinquency and Prevention and Control Act (1961), 49
juvenile incarceration: as black and brown issue, 85–87; as criminalization structure, 83–84; funding for facilities, 78; national statistics, 7, 79; versus resources for education, 81–83. *See also* Stop the Super Jail campaign

Kennedy administration, social policies, 59
Khmer Rouge regime, 110–11, 115
"kid-fixing" model of youth services, 44, 47–48

Larson, Kate, 34–35
Latino/as: effect of deportation on, 117; youth criminalization of, 41–42
Lipsky, Michael, 61–62

Ma, Eve, 60
Ma, Kim Ho, 100, 107
Maira, Sunaina, 17, 99, 107
Matter of Time: Risk and Opportunity in the Nonschool Hours, A (1992), 45, 46–48
Measure K (the Kids First! Initiative), 1, 11, 45, 133n34

Melamed, Jodi, 93–94
memorandum of understanding, 97, 99–100
Mien: immigrant history, 93; police surveillance of, 79
Mitchell, Katharyne, 48
model minority myth, 84–85, 87–88
multiculturalism: limitations of, 92–93; neoliberalism and, 93–94

Nathanson, Constance, 38, 43
Nation at Risk, A (1983), 47
neoliberal governance, 56; deportation as state instrument, 99, 112–14, 118–19; and nonprofits, 5–6, 56–57; voluntary participation of subject, 56–57
neoliberalism, 2–3, 9–10, 56
"non-profit industrial complex," 60, 129
nonprofit organizations: Asian American groups, 92; government contracting with, 59–62; history of, 13–14, 59; neoliberal governance, 5–6, 56–57; nonprofitization, 12, 64–65, 84, 94; role in political economy, 15–16, 62–63
North Bennet Street Industrial School, 31–33, 35–36

Oakland (California): Asian and Pacific Islander demographics, 23–24, 135n73; Black Panthers, 77, 92; government funds for Chinatown, 59; Gray Areas Programs (Ford Foundation), 49, 139–40nn9–10. *See also* Measure K
Office of Community-Oriented Policing Services, 57
Office of Management and Budget, 63–64
Ohlin, Lloyd, 49
Omi, Michael, 63–64
"organic intellectuals," 128

Personal Responsibility and Work Opportunity Reconciliation Act (1966), 98
philanthropy: growth of foundations, 62–63; influence of Carnegie report, 45, 52
Pittman, Karen, 50, 51
Platt, Anthony, 28, 31–32, 37, 39–40
Progressive Era reform, 27–29; against delinquency and sexual immorality, 34–36, 126, 136n5; settlement houses, 30–31; women's role, 32–33; youth delinquency construct, 36–39. *See also* Addams, Jane
Proposition 21 (Gang Violence and Juvenile Crime Prevention Act), 2, 3, 7
Proposition 187, 2, 98

racial identity, depoliticization of, 63–64, 127. *See also* youth of color
Reagan administration, retrenchment of social service programs, 61, 142n72
Rodriguez, Dylan, 14, 87
Rose, Nikolas, 12, 57, 81

"school to prison pipeline," 82–83
second-generation youth, 20
Sentenced Home (2006), 107, 112
September 11: multiracial coalition building after, 117–18; and racialized criminalization, 99
sexual morality: of current-day females, 42–43; of Progressive Era females, 35–39
Shiao, Jay, 63, 64
Smith, Andrea, 88, 127
Smith, Steven, 61–62
Southeast Asian Freedom Network, 103, 117
Southeast Asian refugees, 110–12
Spade, Dean, 127–28
Spirit of Youth and the City Streets, The (Addams), 31
Starr, Ellen, 30–31, 32

Statistical Directive 15 (OMB), 63–64
status offenses: deinstitutionalization of, 42; gendering of, 7, 37–39
"Stop the Super Jail" campaign, 73–74, 76–77
Street Terrorism Enforcement and Prevention Act (1988), 7
Sullivan, Lisa, 53–55, 65, 71
"super-predator," 3, 39–40, 41–42, 80, 138n61; youth of color rejection of, 74, 127

Tax Reform Act (1969), 62
teenage pregnancy, as social problem, 43
Third World movements, 3, 78
Thousand Points of Light program, 19
transgender organizing, 127–28

United States Social Forum, 129–30
Urban Institute, 61–62
Urban Strategies Council, 11

Vietnam, repatriation agreement with, 100
Violent Crime Control and Law Enforcement Act (1994), 57–58
volunteerism, 19–20, 134n61
Volunteers in Service to America, 19–20

War on Poverty programs, 61
Welfare Reform Act (1996), 98
World Social Forum, 129–30

youth: adolescent development research, 29; negative connotations of terminology, 7; power limitations in a representative democracy, 97, 101–2
youth activist groups: foundational funding of, 65–66; nonprofit status of, 12, 64–65
youth crime, decline in, 41–42, 78, 144n19

youth criminalization: challenges by
youth, 74, 127; child protection from,
137n15; differentiated racialization in,
41, 77–79, 90–91; gendering of, 41–
43, 79–80; growing trends, 40–41;
interaction with empowerment policies, 43–44
youth delinquency: female, 35–36, 37–
39, 42–43; male, 7, 37, 38–39; preventive measures, 8–9; statistics on, 7,
41–42. *See also* juvenile court and
justice system; Progressive Era
reform
youth development, 19; positive, 50–52,
123–24; skills, 15, 55; and youth
organizing divide, 15, 67–69, 123–26
Youth Force Coalition, 74

youth incarceration. *See* juvenile
incarceration
Youth Media Council, 103
youth of color: criminalization of justice system and, 41–42; differentiated
racialization within, 90–91; identity
politics, 3, 84–89, 127; police surveillance of, 80
youth organizing, 10; as affirmative
governmentality, 10–11, 119; funding,
54–56, 123–24; as independent
oppositional social movement, 52–
53, 129; participants, 2; and youth
development, 68–69

zero-tolerance crime policies, in
schools, 82–83